INDEPENDENCE IS A STATE OF MIND!

by Nicolette Jacqueline Conway

First printing, 2021.

ISBN:
978-1-80227-085-3 (Paperback)
978-1-80227-086-0 (eBook)

Foreword

I have known Nicki since she was a few months old. Her Mum and I became best friends through our husbands at the time. I'm proud to have Nicki as my Goddaughter. She has always been very strong and determined from a young age, never got frustrated with me when I didn't understand what she wanted but we always managed to get there in the end.

Nicki went away to boarding school to get the best education she could, which has helped her enormously over the years with everything, especially her writing. Even though I didn't see her as much during that time, we would always meet up during school holidays and I would find out about all her new skills she had learned. Nicki and her 2 sisters and my 2 daughters were brought up together, which was lovely because they didn't think of Nicki as being disabled, only as Nicki! This helped them as they got older and they were proud that I was Nicki's Godmother.

As Nicki got older she did her Duke of Edinburgh's award and even abseiled down a small mountain in the Lake District. Going to Bon Jovi concerts, nothing stopped her from doing what she wanted. Her Mother has helped and supported her all the way. It's really hard but Nicki has even done sponsored walks for charity too.

Even when she decided she wanted to live on her own she wasn't discouraged, once again she and her Mum made it happen. Modern technology has helped Nicki to type this book, stay in touch with people and so much more. She has had to learn how to use all the new equipment and we all know how difficult that can be but as usual Nicki has mastered it all.

I have been so proud of Nicki all her life, in all that she has achieved and all that lies ahead of her. She will always put her best foot forward and live life to the full. She puts me to shame. Well done Nicki I can't wait to read your autobiography. Love always Jean

Jean McClaren.

Contents

Abbreviations.

TDS: Thomas de la Rue school
PMC: Princess Marina Centre
CP: Cerebral Palsy
DOE: Duke of Edinburgh's Award
SRSW: Senior Residential Social Worker
OT: Occupational Therapist/Therapy
IYDP: International Year of Disabled Persons
YDH: Young Disabled Holidays
CSV: Community Service Volunteers
CYP: Craig-y-Parc

Acknowledgements

I am dedicating this first part of my autobiography to my Mum, for her endless love, humour, guidance, and dogged perseverance to get me and my sisters everything that we need throughout our lives. I am so grateful for all the advice and some "tough love" I have had over the years. I know I wouldn't have my outlook on life if it hadn't have been for Mum's gentle guidance. Thank you Mum.

Also I would like to acknowledge my speech therapist Ena Davis, who gave me so much encouragement with my eating and communication at the right stage of my life, and remains a very important and trusted person.

I would like to thank all my teachers and houseparents at Craig -y- Parc School, without whom I would not have been taught how to control my body to do things.

I would like to pay tribute to a couple of friends who gave me so much encouragement at the right time of my young adulthood. Colin Bell, who was in my life for such a short time, but his zest for life was infectious.

I was so lucky to have met the inspirational Pat Mitchell, when I was aged 19... Being that much older than me, she really helped me understand how to be a disabled woman, and accept my limitations, but be practical and do things that would make my life easier.

Ian Dury.

I would like to give "a serious nod" to the incredible Ian Dury, for unknowingly inspiring me to be myself no matter what I face in life... I would love his sons, Baxter, Albert and Billy to read this book some day.

The Duke of Edinburgh's Award

I was also lucky enough to do my Gold Duke of Edinburgh's Award as a young adult. I think this scheme was one of the most inspiring periods of my life because I participated in so many activities alongside able bodied people, and this gave me courage to go to an able bodied college and do my exams, and try to do everything I want in life.

Introduction

I hope that people who read my story will find it amusing and enlightening, as I am a happy person. I have always liked to teach and help people in anyway I can, whether it's through raising money or just listening to them.

I have Athetoid Cerebral Palsy, which basically means my body is uncoordinated. Intellectually though, I am all there.

Cerebral Palsy affects a person's ability to control movement, due to the messages from the brain to the muscles getting jumbled up. Cerebral Palsy varies in physical severity, from somebody who is as helpless as a new born baby, through to just a limb being mildly affected.

A few people with Cerebral Palsy have learning difficulties. However, many people with the condition often have above average intellect.

A Cerebral Palsy person can be referred to as a "Spastic"; it is often used in derogatory terms these days. However, I have always used the word "spastic" as it was part of my diagnosis, so I have no issues with the word.

1.

The Conway and Price Families

My maternal grandmother, Rosina Paige was one of 8 children. She was born 31st January 1920, in east London. I can only assume that as she was the eldest and had to assume some responsibility as her siblings arrived in quick succession, because she could never show affection to anyone, although her siblings all were really loving, kind people.

My maternal granddad, Maurice Reuben Price was the only child of his Father's second marriage and was born on 23rd December 1915…He was a lovely, kind man.

Rosina (Rose) and Maurice met as many people do by granddad walking past her house on his way to and from the station at Kingsbury where he got the train into London each day for work. Rose also worked in London so they may have even travelled together sometimes. They married in 1941.

My paternal grandmother, Christian Callender; was from South Shields, Tyne and Wear, Northumbria. She lived in

Lady Close and her sisters Lillian and Sarah and she would have played on the beach of the Tyne. Her mother Mary Frances Welch (formally) knitted shawls for the fishermen's wives. Her Father Nicholas Callender guided the fishing boats through the harbour mouth and into the Tyne River.

In 2009 I had the opportunity to visit me area where nanny Conway grew up and found out People from that particular area are known as Sand Dancers apparently. I remembered a song from the TV series of the 1970s BBC drama serial when the boat comes in, in an arrangement by the composer David Fishawe. I thought I'd look it up and put it in this.

When The Boat Comes In (or *Dance Ti Thy Daddy*) is a traditional English folk song, originating in Northumberland.

The song was also used in the TV advertisement for Young's fish, Sea to Plate campaign.

> *Dance to your Daddy, my little laddy*
> *Dance to your Daddy, my little man*
> *Thou shalt have a fish and thou shalt have a fin*
> *Thou shalt have a codlin when the boat comes in*
> *Thou shalt have haddock baked in a pan*
> *Dance to your Daddy, my little man*
>
> *Dance to your Daddy, my little laddie*
> *Dance to your Daddy, my little man*
> *When thou art a young boy, you must sing and play*
> *Go along the shore and cast your shells away*

Build yourself a castle, watch the tide roll in
Dance to your Daddy, my little man.

Dance to your Daddy, my little laddie
Dance to your Daddy, my little man
When thou art a young man, go unto the trades
Find yourself a skill, and wages you'll be paid
Then with all your wages, buy yourself some land
Dance to your Daddy, my little man

Dance to your Daddy, my little laddie
Dance to your Daddy, my little man
When thou art a man and go to take a wife
Find yourself a lass and love her all your life
She shall be your wife and thou shalt be her man
Dance to your Daddy, my little man

Dance to your Daddy, my little laddie
Dance to your Daddy, my little man
When thou art an old man, father to a son
Sing to him the old songs, sing of all you've done
Pass along the old ways, then let his song begin
Dance to your Daddy, my little man

Christian came down to London in the late 1930's to find work. She got work as a housekeeper for a Jewish family who lived Golders Green.

A romance developed between the housekeeper and gardener. John Conway married Christian Callender in September 1940.

Nanny Conway was a simple, kind lovely lady, and figures a lot in my childhood...

I love the Geordie accent now; I'm not sure if it is because of Nanny Conway, or because I have met a lot of really smashing people from Northumbria. Three people in particular, apart from nanny.

I never knew my paternal Grandfather John Conway who was of Irish descent and one of his ancestors was a tiler and worked in the Blackwall tunnel that runs under the Thames from Tower Hamlets to Greenwich peninsula...

He was conscripted into the army in the Second World War. He didn't see active service as he got stationed at Scapa Flow in Scotland.

Then in the 1950's he worked for John Laing the builders as a gardener at their offices in Mill Hill north London.

My parents...

I will start my story in Golders Green, North London. Early 1945 and World War II was still raging over the suburb. Luckily it was the baby's feed time and so Rose picked up her first baby girl from her cot... Suddenly the house shook with a Boom from a Doodlebug bomb that had exploded a quarter of a mile away. Rose Price didn't like girl babies. So it was just luck that Rose picked up little Jacqueline Frances from her cot as the force from the bomb had shattered the window beside the cot, filling it.

Mum has 3 brothers, Arne, Kenneth and Peter. My granddad was an electrician in the print. He worked at The Mirror in Fleet Street in London for a time, so he was quite respected in his trade.

He also worked in Africa at one stage setting up the printing press in Lagos, in Nigeria. He wasn't very happy that he was given a servant.

As a child, I always remember granddad having a lot of African ornaments around his flat in Cricklewood. I had a favourite ornament of all of them, a bust of an African lady. It wasn't very big but I thought she was pretty.

The Family home was Spur road, on a new housing estate in Edgware north London.

The young Queen Elizabeth II opened the new estate in about 1958. It was a major news event and Mum can remember all the children who lived on the estate had the day off school to watch the unveiling of a plaque.

My Nan left granddad when Mum was 13, and married a man called Ben Holmes, and had another two children called Vanessa and Vernon... Nan and Ben were labour party supporters. They were also Masons at one point. Having just read about the Masons I am surprised that Ben was allowed in the front door, as he had no morals and was in no way understanding or charitable.

My Mum was always really clever with her hands and went to Kilburn polytechnic aged 13, to learn a trade. After trying various skills she decided to train as an Upholsteress. She worked hard and over the next few years learnt her trade to a high standard. When she left the technical college in 1961 she worked in London at W.F. Atkins near Marble Arch as an Upholsteress. Where she continued to learn more and work on high class furnishings for the lords and ladies of high society and some of the royals.

Mum and granddad were very close because of the lack of contact and love from Rose. Mum didn't have contact with her mother until she had to get permission to marry Dad, as in those days the age of consent was 21.

My Dad, Micheal John Conway, was born at home, Layfield Crescent, West Hendon, London, in June 1944. My Dad was the middle son of three. He had an elder brother called Richard (Uncle Dick) who was born in 1941 during the war. And then Christian had another son, my uncle Peter, in 1947.

I know very little about my Dad's childhood. I can only remember him talking about one thing that happened to him when he was a little boy. Nanny had made a pot of porridge for the boys and had left it too close to the edge of the table. Dad was an inquisitive toddler and decided to reach up to get the pot that smelt so yummy. The pot tipped upside-down and the porridge burnt his chest. He had the scars for the rest of his life. I know it was an accident, but it makes me cringe to think about it!!

My granddad, John Conway died in 1957. Aged 38. Christian had no choice but to work to support her three boys and herself. She went back to work as a housekeeper in Golders Green and remained a loyal servant to two Jewish families up until about six months prior to her death in 1990.

Dad left school when he was 15 and did decorating. Then he trained to be an instrument polisher at Boosey and Hawkes, Dad loved the skill of polishing the orchestral instruments.

In 1961, Mum's best mate Jean Barker, asked her to go on a night out. There was going to be a big crowd of youngsters from London gathered at Mill Hill, and it would be a laugh… Michael John Conway and Jacqueline Frances Price met that night. She was 16 and he was 17. Just kids in the midst of the Mods and Rockers era, and the sexual revolution… They didn't get together until sometime later because they were seeing other people at the time. Mum has told me that Dad looked quite dapper, in his powder blue drain pipe jeans, white shirt and brown Chelsea boots when she saw him on that night.

My parents had to be different. As my Mum described it, they were "Hippy Mods, with a motorbike fetish". Dad couldn't stand scooters. He called them "Farts on wheels"! I always remember him saying that when he saw or heard one. He loved big motorbikes, especially big English bikes!!

There was always music and motorbikes at home. A great combination… My parents had a varied taste in music which included Fleetwood Mac, The Bee-Gees, Buddy Holly, The Who, Elvis, The Beatles. The Rolling Stones and The Moody Blues

Only being 18, Mum was under the age of consent so she had to get permission to marry from her mother, even though Rose had not been in contact with her for 5 years.

Their relationship was never close, although they stayed in touch for the next 50 years.

My parents, Michael John Conway and Jacqueline Frances Price, married on October 12th 1963, at Burnt Oak registry office Edgware. Mum told me that it was a lovely sunny day and a blue tit flew onto the balcony of their flat just before she left to go to the registry office. Granddad drove her in his blue and white Austin Cambridge car!!! Mum is only 5ft 1" and I think Dad was only 5ft4" on their wedding day. He continued to grow until he was 21, I think he was 5"7" eventually.

Mum's dress had fleecy lined bodice. This amused me when Mum told me because she is always cold but the thought of a fleece bodice of a wedding dress conjured up funny images. When they arrived at Brighton on their honeymoon they found Kippers in their suitcase. Mum really hates fish, and is allergic to it.

After having an electric shock Granddad lost his sense of smell. Mum has always told me how she would worry that when she left home to live in her marital home, that she would find really rank food in his fridge when she visited him. She often found food that was too far gone over date.

2.

My Early Years

I was born on December 27th 1963 at the Whittington Hospital in Islington, North London. Dick Whittington is supposed to have heard the bells of Bow where the hospital stands, calling him to be Mayor of London. So I am actually a cockney! Mum was only 19 when she had me. The doctor wasn't even at my birth, just a male midwife. Mum told me that when she was giving birth she was biting on her hand but couldn't understand why she couldn't feel anything. She was biting hard on the nurse's hand!!

I was about three weeks late being born and there were complications with my birth; I was a Breech baby and my mum had to be induced. There was a new experimental drug to bring babies on and the doctor was using it on a lot of mothers... The drug brought me on too quickly and I got stuck halfway out of Mum and I died. Then when they had revived me I was put into an incubator which pumped oxygen into me,

I had tubes going into everywhere. My poor Mum was still on the bed where I had been born and could see everything that they were doing. The lack of Oxygen for three quarters of an hour caused me to suffer a major brain haemorrhage, leaving extensive damage to the cerebellum part of my brain, causing me to have severe Cerebral Palsy. AKA CP

I was christened the night I was born because I wasn't expected to live through the night. I was christened by a Catholic priest because my father, Michael John, was of that faith, although he wasn't practicing. My Mum was in no fit state to say what religion she wanted me to be, that night. My full name is Nicolette Jacqueline Conway. Most people call me Nicki. I was in hospital for 6 weeks after my birth because I had jaundice and ulcers on my eyes. My Mum decided to have me christened again when I came home. Mum was practicing Church of England and didn't know anything about the Catholic faith.

Mum had so much to learn, it's amazing how she coped with me when I was a baby. Mum didn't realise why I had no control over my mouth. I couldn't even take a bottle because I don't have the sucking reflex. Mum cup fed me drinks right from a baby. It would take hours to feed me! I have Tongue Thrusts, which is where the tongue comes forward in spasm. I can't control my mouth and so I lose a lot of food. My Mum used to have to smack me to get me crying, so as I gulped for air the food would go down. My uncle Arne would call Mum all the cruel bitches under the sun, but that was literally the

14

only way she could get me eating. - I love my food now, and I am a bit of a gannet to say the least!!! There were no help groups for Mum to contact for advice and social services were very little help.

The Whittington Hospital never admitted to Mum or Dad just how bad my brain damage had been.

We have found out that a few other children born under the same Doctor have C.P. He was found dead on Hampstead Common sometime after my birth.

There was no enquiry into my birth, even though there were obvious serious mistakes made. Dad was a very private person and couldn't have coped with the attention that would have occurred. I don't think my parents ever thought of seeking financial compensation as it wasn't acknowledged that Cerebral Palsy could be prevented. I think I am lucky because I do not have much money and appreciate everything that I have and do, or receive.

I know on one hand money can't buy happiness, but I would have been financially independent for life and wouldn't have to be as frugal.

Home life.

Mum and Dad were living in a bed sit, in Bishops Avenue, Highgate, London; when 1 arrived into the world. Nanny Conway wasn't happy about that and so it was decided that we would move back into her house, in Mill Hill, North London.

Nanny had a 3 bed roomed semi detached council house, on a bit of a hill. From seeing photos I think the garden was big with a coal shed, lawn and had a baby swing and frame in. Back then, there were fields at the end of the garden. I expect that has all been built on now.

Mum has told me that she had a lot of people ridicule her because they thought Mum was letting me stay in the pram when I was obviously old enough to walk. She said the butcher in Woodcoat Avenue told her that I was lazy and should be made to walk. One day Mum was sick of his gibes and told him that I was a Spastic and couldn't do anything for myself. As politically incorrect as that statement is now, it stopped his comments dead.

My Mum always understood me, and saw that I had a brain. She tells me that when I was about two, or three, I would look at the clock at six o'clock, and then look up. Which meant, as Zebbidy (from the Magic Roundabout children's programme in the 1960's) would say, time for bed! This was a very simple form of communication but very effective!!! I still use this form of communication for many different things because it is the easiest and quickest.

If a carer is clued up on nonverbal communication, they just click into my life and it's very easy to care for me. Unfortunately I have to put up with a lot of carers who don't have that certain instinct and that is frustrating.

Children have funny little quirks and I was no exception. I was frightened of flowers Mum told me that I would cry if anyone put me near them. I love flowers now and anything to do with nature.

I remember I thought nuns could fly... I have no idea where I got that idea from and I am going to get so much stick if I ever published this book!! I was only a baby.. Mum has told me that nuns used to come round to the house and try to convert Mum to the Catholic faith.

When I was a baby Dad's youngest brother, my Uncle Peter was aged 19, still lived at home and he became like my big brother. He was a loveable rogue who mucked around with everyone and of course he would tease me.

I vaguely remember being sat propped up on a sofa in front of the big black and white TV, watching my favourite program Top of the pops.

I liked Peter Noone because he always smiled at me! (I thought) I remember Uncle Peter would stand in front of the T.V. blocking my view, especially if Peter Noone came on!! I would laugh and go crazy at him. Music is very important to me. Even as a baby I loved music.

Another singer/TV presenter/artist that I liked as a child and continued to watch and admire was Rolf Harris. I vividly remember watching his Saturday evening entertainment shows on TV and loving his huge paintings that he did. I don't know whether I was subconsciously inspired to paint like him, but a lot of my paintings turn out like his.

In the 1990's Rolf showed his artistic talent by presenting a series of programmes where he painted in the style of a past masters. I really enjoyed the Van Gough programme and liked Rolf's "Starry Night"!

Another time he painted the nicest portraits of Queen Elizabeth II, that I had seen in a long time.

I was very disappointed when the news came out about his and other "Celebrities of the 1960/70's" exploits of all those poor girls, in 2014. I know other people were very angry and disillusioned with the Yew tree investigation and subsequent convictions. Those poor children.

My Cousins.

I had a small paternal family and I am the eldest of my generation on my Dad's side.

Dad had an elder brother called Dick. He had got married before I was born and so I don't have any vivid memories of him at this age. Dick's wife was called Chris and she was my God mother. She was very pretty

He divorced Chris, I vaguely remember Dick living in a townhouse, I remember this because Dad had to carry me up stairs to Dick's living room.

Dick and Chris remarried, and then had Simon and Elaine in the 1970's.

Dad's younger brother, my Uncle Peter met and married a nice lady called Gill. I think my two youngest cousins, Mark and Tim, were born quite soon thereafter. The Conway family are not very close, I don't know why.

I have a big maternal family and I'm the second eldest of my first cousins. Andrew is six months older than me. He is Arne and Jean's son. They also had Julia and Diane later on.

We were close to my uncle Kenny and Pat, and their children Debbie, Paula (and her snotty nose)... and Billy. Debbie and I were about the same age and so we would play together up in our bedroom.

And just to confuse matters, Mum's youngest brother Peter met and married a lady called Gill, in about 1982. Gill was from Yorkshire and their wedding was in the winter. I remember it snowed on their wedding day. I think I fell in love with the Yorkshire landscape that day!

A couple of years later they had a son called Matthew. Matthew is now 6ft+, married with a little girl.

Mum started getting really worried about me when I was about 18 months old because I wasn't making any attempt to do the things that a child at that age would normally do, like starting to talk, walk and crawl, and explore the world around me.

Mum was taking me regularly to the baby clinic where up until this time all they would say was,

"Oh she has had a bad start, what do you expect. She'll catch up!".

Eventually the Doctor at the clinic decided

"Maybe there is something wrong with Nicki"!!

He then referred me to a special centre in London. I first went to Cheyne Walk centre in Chelsea, Chelsea embankment, London when I was 18 months old.

Cheyne Walk was an Infant school and an assessment centre. I was referred to the Head Doctor there, Dr Foley. He was a tall, very thin and, to me; a scary man who specialised in this type of work.

Doctor Foley took one look at me, pulled the skin on the back of my hand up a little and told Mum bluntly;

"She has severe Cerebral Palsy".

He also told Mum that I would not reach maturity...

Nanny Conway went with Mum. The two women had no idea what Cerebral Palsy was, they sat there stunned. My Dad had gone to work because neither of my parents expected to be told that anything drastic was wrong with me.

Obviously the Dr. at the baby clinic had some inclination of what was wrong with me to send us to Cheyne Walk in the first place.

If I had been born about twenty-years earlier, I would have been put into an institution and probably considered to be an idiot cripple. If I was born twenty-years later however, Mum would have been given a caesarean, and if there was still something wrong with me, Mum and Dad could get advice from her solicitor about negligence...

As it was, I had my diagnosis in May 1965 and just started attending Cheyne Walk School for physiotherapy that June. I also began my nursery class education then.

Cheyne Walk is in Chelsea, Embankment, in central London

The building's frontage was Victorian with steps up to the entrance. There was no such thing as wheelchair access in those days, the children were carried up the steps or bumped up in pushchairs and wheelchairs.

There was a small residential unit attached to Cheyne Walk School and some of the children slept there during the week.

3.

My Infant School Years

$\cdot\!\!\!\!+\!\!\!\!\!\rightarrow\!\!\!\!*\!\!\!\!\leftarrow\!\!\!\!+\cdot$

My first Physiotherapist was called Monica Brewer, she was brown-curly haired and cuddly, she always seemed the same. She was a very dedicated lady and gave my Mum and Dad a hell of a lot of support throughout my childhood.

The only drawback was that she a problem with her bodily odour. Mum tells me 1 would start to gag when she was treating me. I'm still sensitive to smells, if 1 can smell somebody 1 will do everything 1 can not to go too near them. Another thing 1 hate but have to put up with is, if people have garlic for their dinner the night before and then get me up the next morning. It's awful having somebody with bad breath to get you up. However, as every disabled person will know; this is just something you have to put up with.

Mum came to Cheyne Walk with me every day. She went into the house parents' room while I had my physiotherapy and did sewing for the children who stayed at Cheyne Walk during the week. One of the house parents Frosty, also had a disabled child, advised Mum to do whatever Dr Foley recommended for me. Even having more children...

While I wasn't having Physiotherapy, I went into Miss Sayer's nursery class. I can't remember what we did in Miss Sayer's class. I know that we had afternoon naps on little camp beds with our names on the top, and I think Miss Sayer read a story.

I remember Mum teaching me to read with a big letter book. I can't remember learning the alphabet though. The way I learnt to read was phonetically, which was the preferred teaching method in the 1960s. I can't remember much about actually learning to read but I remember Mum knew if I was "saying" the right word.

I have a vague memory of being shown a book of words in the garden class and getting praised for putting my hand up. I don't like maths at all. My brain just doesn't work very well with numerously. Although I know if something is expensive and I keep my financial affairs in check, as much as I can because of my reliance on carers.

PETO

When I was 3 or 4 I went into the Garden class, which was downstairs and opened onto the playground.

Miss Brewer went to Budapest to find out about a new Physiotherapy method, PETO.

PETO, now also known as Conductive Education was developed by the Hungarian physician, András Petö, in Budapest in the years immediately following World War II.

He started an institute for children in Hungary to have intense PETO method.

Its aim is to help children and adults with motor disorders learn to overcome problems of movement as a way of enabling them to live more active and independent lives.

Mum was thinking about taking me to Hungary to go to the PETO institute, but she fell pregnant with my sister Sharon so she decided not to uproot the family.

Miss Brewer and a lady called Mrs Cotton started a PETO class at Cheyne Walk and I was put into it when I was five. I think that was the very first conductive education class in England.

I didn't like this new class because it was hard work! You had to sit on these chairs called "ladder backs", which were wooden, and hard on my bum. I was a skinny kid and am not that much fatter now.

Every day, after lunch I would have to put the bibs into a bucket ready to go to the laundry. All I can remember about this is having a pile of bibs on the table in front of me, a bucket on the floor beside me and knocking the bibs off the table in the general direction of the bucket! I don't think I was a very good shot somehow

I remember being put beside a boy called Kevin to do this, he had blonde hair and was more able than me.

I was a bit of a rebel even then and used to be naughty! I was put outside the classroom for disturbing the others quite a few times.

I am not sure how I disrupted the class as I can't do much. I probably just made lots of noises and didn't co-operate with the teachers

Dr. Foley took film of all the children at Cheyne Walk. So there is some film of me all through my childhood, to show my physical development. (or the lack of it)! Dr Foley had a big room high up in the building, you could see across the Thames from the window. There were a lot of film studio lights, which made me hot. Miss Brewer would be filmed as she exercised me. I didn't like being filmed when I was little because it was hot and hard work. Mum always came up to the room when I was being filmed.

All infant schools have Christmas parties and Father Christmas and Cheyne Walk was no exception. I remember loving the Christmas parties at Cheyne Walk because they were upstairs in Miss Sayer's class. I couldn't eat the jelly because it just doesn't stay in my mouth. I have sort of a dislike for it anyway. I was fascinated by Father Christmas though and loved it when he came along with his sack loaded with presents.

I don't remember having speech therapy at this age but I think a lady called Holly was the Occupational Therapist. She was a really nice lady and became friendly with Mum and I think I was one of her bride's maids. I seem to remember I wore a little yellow dress like the other bride's maids. I didn't walk down the aisle behind Holly, just had my photo taken with her and her husband.

I have no memories of having speech therapy here. Mum tells me that the Speech therapist used to try to calm my tongue thrusts down by putting ice on my tongue and lips. Evidently ice acts like an anaesthetic which calms the spasms down. Although I have never found this to work when I have asked carers to give me an ice lolly.

Mum went into Cheyne Walk with me every day. Until my sister Sharon was born when l was nearly three years old. Shortly followed by my other sister Michelle, when l was four and a half. Nanny Holmes came into school with me when Mum had the babies, although I don't remember her doing so. Mum really had her hands full with baby Michelle, Sharon just a toddler, and me, as dependent as a baby! Dad was in work and didn't help with us girls.

When Michelle came along and I got a little older, I was picked up by taxi from home to go to Cheyne Walk, I don't remember much about the taxi. All I remember of the taxi was that we picked up a girl called Natasha who lived on to other side of the golf course. I always liked that name and I have written a few children stories, and have named one of my main characters Natasha.

My first "friend" that 1 can remember was a day girl with me at the centre, we also shared a taxi at one point. Her name is Linda Robertson, from Cricklewood in London. We stayed together all through school although she had a slight learning disability. .

Family and Home life.

Swimming is brilliant Physiotherapy and when I was very little, we went swimming on Tuesday evenings at Swiss Cottage in London. My instructor nick-named me "Tadpole" because I was really small. I don't know his name, but he was a really good instructor and made me work hard. I can't swim at all. For some reason I just sink!!

There was a lady called Peggy who insisted on pinching my nose. This would have been funny if I had been an able-bodied kiddie but as I can't breathe through my mouth, it was a bit dangerous. Peggy wouldn't just give my nose a quick gentle pinch either, she'd pinch really hard and make me cry! Mum always gently told her off but Peggy didn't understand why it was wrong.

Sharon and Michelle came with us. We would always have a hot Ribena to drink after swimming…

I can't remember how old I when we got a puppy and Mum called her Mandy. She was a Heinz-57 cross Corgi and German shepherd. She was short and had the face like a German shepherd's face; she was such a lovely dog.

When Mum used to assist me to walk around the house, Mandy would jump up and put her paws on my waist and pull me down. She just thought I shouldn't walk around. We would all laugh and Mandy would be happy that I was safely on the floor with her.

I loved Christmas as a child. Mum would put the decorations up on Christmas Eve and then wrap all our presents up. We woke up to a pillow case full of sweets, fruit and a few presents on the bottom of our beds. Sharon and Michelle would help me open my presents in bed.

When Mum and Dad got up, we would all go downstairs where the sitting room would all decorated and have loads of presents laid in rows from Santa for us all.

Granddad Price and Nanny Conway seemed to come to us every Christmas time.

The only day I didn't like was Boxing Day afternoon, because we went over to Nanny Holmes' place for Christmas tea and a family get together. It was nice to see my aunties and uncles, and all my cousins.

My cousin Diane, has told me that she remembers reading aloud to me when she was learning to read and write. I would have been about 9 and she would have been about 4. I probably told Mum if she got a word wrong.

Nan and Ben lived above the shops at Queensbury, north London. It was a weird marriage and it had no love in it. Nan lived in the dining room and Ben lived in the front room.

The cousins didn't like Ben I have found out recently so I wasn't the only one.

He had a son who was learning disability and had passed away. Ben wouldn't accept that I am not like his son. He always talked to me very loudly and patronisingly; he always wanted me to sit on his lap... And he smoked huge cigars that stank. I hate smelly cigars now!!

I can't talk but I can get sounds out. For instance I'd say "en" instead of Ben. Most people would be really pleased that I try to say their name. However this awful man wouldn't accept this and shout "Not en.. BBen"!

I would get angry at him and grit my teeth at him. Mum would be annoyed with him and take me away from him and put me with my sisters and cousins.

The next day is my birthday. I would have lots of people come to see me on my birthday. Mum would also take me and my sisters out somewhere special as well. I remember going to see Disney on ice, at Wembley arena for one birthday. I wore an orange trouser suit that I had got for either Christmas or birthday.

The other person who just couldn't understand my disability was my Great Aunty Anne. She was an innocent gem. She just didn't understand physical disability and she would talk to me like l was a baby, she would tell Sharon and

Michelle off when it was me who had started the arguing and being naughty. Aunty and Uncle Will lived down in Ramsgate and we would go to see them every so often. On one visit we went for a walk, 1 can remember it was a nice sunny day and aunty decided to buy us three girls an ice cream. Mum told her not to buy me one as it was difficult to feed me out, so aunty brought me a present. (I was about 13, Sharon 10 and Michelle 8) I was at the age where like all teenagers, 1 liked to look "grown up". Aunty Anne returned with this bag and in it was a toy, she opened it and said

"I thought you would like this,"

Pulling out a bright yellow rubber duck, saying

"it's a ducky.."

Of course, Mum, Dad Sharon and Michelle were wetting themselves with laughter because 1 was looking at this thing in total disbelief. I think Mum took it and made out 1 was trying to say Thank you, when 1 was really saying

"Oh no 1 don't believe it! What the bloody hell is it! I'm not a kid!"

Mum, Sharon and Michelle have teased me ever since about "Rubber Duckies".

Looking back on this now, I know that Aunty Anne just didn't have any concept of disability. After all, in her young days, disabled people were put into big institution and not seen.

I have got about five little plastic yellow ducks now in my bathroom just as a little reminder of Auntie Anne.

In 1970, I was aged six; I went to be assessed at (as it was then) The Spastic Society's headquarters, Park Crescent, London. All I can remember about this assessment is being asked to find the doll, which was amongst some objects on a table. I looked at Mum as if to say "is he serious"? Then looked directly at the doll, and laughed!

I had to change schools when I turned seven because I was considered to be highly educable at the assessment.

Mum and Dad wanted me to carry on with the PETO method because I was improving quite a lot physically.

The only school in Britain that was doing PETO at this time was Craig y Parc, in Cardiff. After a lot of discussions with Mum I decided to go away from Mum and Dad, to this school. I think I looked upon it as a big adventure, and after all I had stayed at Nanny Conway's quite often and Mum and Dad always came back for me..

I don't know who it was but a social worker called Mum all the cruel bitches under the sun, because she was sending her seven-year-old daughter away to school. Albeit, it was me who had made the decision to go away to school, which I don't regret at all. I don't think I'd be as independently minded as I am now if I'd stayed at home.

4.

Craig -y- Parc School.

The family home was in Whetston, North London. We had a golf course backing onto our garden and the golf balls often got putted over the trees into the garden. Had we been older, Sharon and Michelle and I could have made an absolute fortune by selling the golf balls back to the golfers!!

When I was about five years old, Dad broke his arm on a polishing machine at Boosey and Hawkes. It was quite a serious break as he had to have two plates in his wrist, he could no longer rotate his wrist properly so he could no longer be a skilled instrument polisher so he left B&H. He loved being a skilled polisher.

He wasn't happy and went back to Boosey and Hawkes to work as an unskilled polisher.

Dad was a perfectionist, and couldn't cope with being an unskilled polished and became demoralised, which eventually lead to depression.

He would bring a few of the imperfect instruments home and we have still got them. I assume that they were not quite right and so couldn't go for orchestra use.

I have got a Bugle that Dad polished hanging in my sitting room and carers often comment on it.

Boarding school life.

In the February of 1971 I went away to Craig -y- Parc School near Cardiff. I was meant to start there in January but my second cousin Mark went down with meningitis, so the whole family was put in quarantine for about six weeks. Mark recovered and we resumed normal life.

I was seven, Sharon was four and Michelle was three. Michelle doesn't remember me being at home all the time, and going to day school.

Nanny Conway had given me two dolls to go away with. I called them Ann and Frosty. Nearly all my dollies were called Ann because that was all 1 could say! I named the other one Frosty after my favourite house parent at Cheyne Walk.

Sharon always vomited on the way back to Cardiff, she wasn't normally travelsick but it was the event of the journey. Mum could never understand why Sharon was sick, but had loads of plastic bags with her!

The M4 wasn't finished when we first started going to Cardiff and so it would take us hours to get to Cardiff.

We would have to drive West on the A40 from the family home in Whetstone, all the way to Pentyrch in Wales. It must have taken hours going through all the towns, including Mill Hill, Watford, Aylesbury, Oxford, Cheltenham, Chipping-Sodbury, Bath, and lots of little villages before Bristol. The M4 had just been built from Bristol to Cardiff via the River Severn toll bridge, Newport, Radyr and finally Pentyrch.

The journey took about 4 hours so I was lucky only having to do it one way, the rest of my family had to return home.

The River Severn toll bridge is about a mile wide and I remember I liked going over the Severn toll bridge because you could see for miles. The river banks are mud flats so it is good for seabirds.

When I started going to Craig –y- Parc I would get upset when we got near to Pentyrch because I would miss my Mum and Dad and sisters. To cheer me up and keep my mind off of school, we'd play "I spy".

I remember, Michelle had us going crazy on one journey. She was only about four and she said "I spy something beginning with T"!! We went through everything we could see... Trousers? No! Tops? No! Tongue? No! Trees? No... We could not get this thing so we gave up. With a big grin, Michelle pointed at the dashboard and said "Tewing gum"!!! We all cracked up!

School Life.

Craig -y- Parc was built in the style of a big 17ᵗʰ century stone mansion at the top of a hill. The road up to the school was windy and narrow; Dad had to toot the car horn on every bend.

Eventually you came to a gatehouse, and then you drove up a long drive at the front of this great big, lead light windowed mansion. At the top of the drive was a circle of grass with an oak tree in the middle. The main entrance to the school had stone steps up to a big wooden door. The front of the mansion had three parts, with triangle roofs.

Along the drive were new buildings, these were the classrooms, assembly hall, and therapy rooms.

In those days, the grounds were kept immaculate by one gardener. An old man seemed to be the only employed gardener. The older, able boys used to work in the gardens.

The view from the back of the mansion was spectacular, you could see for miles!

The gardens were huge. There was a long terraced garden, which stepped down for about a quarter of a mile. At the top of the terraced gardens was an old style stone summerhouse. The gardens were not really wheelchair accessible but the house parents and teachers would take us round the gardens and bump us up and down the steps. Obviously this was before the European legislation about back injury came in.

One of the classrooms was in the old part. This classroom was away from the mansion, only adjoined to the mansion by a roof. There was a little lane leading up to this classroom, from the road from Pentyrch.

Craig –y- Parc was surrounded by woods and fields. It was absolutely beautiful, remembering it now, but we didn't appreciate it as kids. Although I remember I loved the spring there because we could see the lambs running and jumping about from the classroom.

Mrs Kerslake, the headmistress, was a tall, thin lady. She was very strict and ran the school with a tight reign. On that first day, I think Mum and Dad had to give her all my details.

When Mum and Dad had gone a house parent took me down to the PETO group for my tea.

I don't remember getting upset because they had left me at the school but I probably did after tea.

I can't imagine how Mum felt as they all drove away from Craig –y- Parc. She has told me that she would go to sleep when she left me at boarding school, all the way home. And wouldn't go into my bedroom at home until just before I returned.

Debbie.

I met a little ginger haired girl called Debbie Sherrington, I think I was sat next to her on my first tea time there. Debbie was six and I had just turned seven. We hit it off straight away and we had no problems communicating whatsoever, we became friends almost from that day.

Debbie can't walk and the best way she got about was to shuffle along on her bottom and boy could she shift! Debbie can talk and use her hands so basically she became my mouth and hands.

When Debbie and I were little, we had our own way of talking, which went like this. Debbie would ask me a question like, "Would you like a sweet"? I would either nod or shake my head as necessary.

This was OK as long as I didn't want to tell her anything, then what happened was Debbie would say the alphabet, then I would nod my head when she said the right letter, and so on until we built up the words of the sentence that I wanted to tell her.

As we got older we wanted to speed that up, we split the alphabet up into two halves, and she asks me "first or second", if I say first, she then recites ABC..... But if I say second, she then recites NOPQR...... We still do this now, and it totally baffles people when we are in company.

The house parents forgot to explain to me that there was a big quarry down the road from Craig -y- Parc and I can remember being really frightened on my first night. I heard this great big boom that came from outside, and I just didn't know what it was. I think I started crying for Mum and so after she told me what this great big boom was, Jean Brown, the house parent; put me in the bed next to Debbie's.

From that day on, we became best friends. Jean also put my two dolls beside me.

The PETO Unit.

The PETO unit was in the new building and we had two main classrooms, a dining room, 2 dormitories and a carer sleep in room.

The dormitories had about 6 beds in each and we had a locker beside our bed.

The beds were metal tubular framed so that the children could hold on to stand up when necessary. But we had normal mattresses to sleep on. Unlike at the PETO institute in Hungary where the children slept on wooden plinths so they had to lie straight all night. Thank God Mum fell pregnant with Sharon when she did, or I would have been taken out there.

Every week a night nurse from the main house would come down and leave sweets on every child's locker. I often would wake up and she'd take me to the loo and I would get sweet, usually a smarty!!

One of the first people to bring the PETO method to England was a lady called Mrs Cotton. She was very strict and I knew her from Cheyne Walk. I just didn't like Mrs Cotton and I hated it when she came down from London and slept in because she wasn't very motherly and she'd just make us go to bed and be quiet. When the house parents slept in they'd read us a story or let us play games until 7.00.

We didn't sit in wheelchairs at all in the PETO unit; instead we had to sit on wooden chairs without arms or belts to secure us. This was to make us use our core strength and become physically independent.

The chairs were called Ladder backed chairs and were really hard on my skinny little butt.

I couldn't sit by myself for a long period of time. I just don't have the balance. Miss Magor had some wooden arms put on my chair and I think she put a strap around my waist.

It was quite a homely atmosphere at Craig –y- Parc and the teachers in the PETO unit were nice. When I went to Craig –y- Parc the teachers were Miss Magor and Mrs James, they taught basic English, maths, RE and geography.

Mrs Easterbrooke, was the full time physiotherapist, and we had two House parents called Jean Brown and Chris Pizzie.

These two house parents were my first experience of having carers and I had a lot to learn. Fortunately they were nice and did actually care about the children.

One day as we were getting ready for bed when Debbie pulled a chest of drawers on top of herself as she held onto the handles trying to stand up. She was OK but she was upset and frightened. I saw it happen and I was upset about her. I think the house parents sat Debbie on my bed and let us play our dolls for a little while.

I enjoyed the class time and my reading continued to improve. Miss Magor had the knack of understanding the children who had no speech when they "read aloud".

We had the Ladybird books "Peter and Jane" to read from, I can remember liking the stories and smiling at Miss Magor when she came to hear me read to her.

I remember when the UK changed currency from imperial to decimal. I don't think I found it difficult because I hadn't had to handle money before. Miss Magor taught maths too, but I didn't get on very well. I am still not very good with numbers.

The school had 2 dogs in the seven years that I attended. The first one, Prince, was a Rough Collie. He was beautiful and really placid with the kids. He had long fir, which must have been pulled so many times through the children's' hand spasming when they stroked him. He got old and died, I don't know whether he had to be put down or if he died from natural causes, but he was put in the school's pet crematory.

A little while after, Mrs Kerslake got a Border Collie puppy called Sheba. I don't remember much about Sheba but having a Border Collie myself, I know that she would have been a brilliant dog to be a special school's dog. Border Collies are so intelligent and they seem to be caring. It's amazing!!

I have one memory of Sheba. We were queuing to go up in the lift in the main house and along came the puppy, she squatted and then she crapped in the middle of the lift floor!!

I remember it was quite a loose and smelly one!! The house parents had to clean it up, much to the amusement of us kids

Home life.

Dad received an industrial injury payout and so the family moved to Borehamwood quite soon after I went to my new school. Mum and Dad actually told the council that we were swapping houses with my uncle Peter and aunty Gill. They didn't actually swap houses; Dad just paid the rent on Peter's flat for a month and then gave it up. This gave Peter and family a house with a nice garden.

Our new house was a three bed roomed semi detached new build house, in Lexington close, Borehamwood, Hertfordshire. Situated about 15 miles north of London,

Borehamwood had the ATV studios and film studios from the 1920s onwards, the town became known as one of the main centres of the UK film, and later television, industries due to the presence of production studios

Since the 1920s, the town has been home to several film studios and many shots of its streets are included in final cuts of 20th century British films.

Many well-known movies including Cliff Richard's "The Young Ones" and "Summer Holiday", "Dr Zhivago", " The Confessions of.... series of films", *2001: A Space Odyssey*, *Moby Dick*, *The Dam Busters*, *633 Squadron*, *The Shining* starring

Jack Nicholson. All that remains of the original studio, which has been much reduced in size and usefulness to production companies as a result. Elstree Studios where, more recently used for, BBC TV's most popular soap, EastEnders and their popular medical drama Holby City. The studio has also been used for Question Time. And probably the BBC's biggest success ever, Strictly Come Dancing is filmed there.

I take most of my carers to Boreham wood so they can see where Eastenders is made now. You can't see much of the set, but we go along Stratford road and see the back of "the square". It's not very exciting but the foreign ladies like it.

A lot of the cast live in the area and you often see them in Borehamwood high Street. I saw Pam St Clement, Eastenders "Pat Wicks/Butcher", in the London Colney Sainsbury's, one day but that is all.

The walls in our new house were very thin and we often heard the neighbours sneeze. Bizarrely the house had a pig farm right next door. The close was only separated from the farm by a wooden fence. Our house was right beside the farm and we often would get wafts of pigs.

We had a pretty big garden for a new build. It was big enough for Dad to build a pretty big patio, and we had a good size lawn. Dad also dug quite a big fishpond and rockery.

It was an open plan sitting room and dining room. The stairs went up from the sitting room.

Upstairs there was a big bedroom, a smaller bedroom and a tiny box room which was my bedroom.

Dad decorated my bedroom and built a cabin bed for me. I had pink and purple floral wallpaper! (It was the 70s) I think we had mustard coloured carpet all through the house. I was allowed to have posters pinned to polystyrene squares stuck on the wall above my bed. One of the posters had pink sepia pictures of Elton John, Gilbert O'Sullivan, Mark Boland and David Essex surrounding a big colour picture of Donny Osmond. It was an odd collection of people because they didn't perform the same sort of music at all.

Sharon started school at Maryfield primary school; she had to wear a school uniform. Michelle went to the same school a year later.

Mum had been a stay at home Mum all the first years of our lives, and I am sure she was happy to be this. However, she was a brilliant upholsteress

She got a part time job at HPB at Elstree aerodrome and did 9-3 so she was always there for Sharon and Michelle when they came out of school, and to have Dad's dinner on the table at six O'clock.

Elstree aerodrome is about 3 miles away from Borehamwood and became one of London's private airfields after World War II.

HPB re-upholstered executive planes and so the work was always top quality and excellent...

We sometimes went into work with Mum and the boss let us use one of the offices as a playroom. We took dolls, doll prams, bikes, Roller boots and anything we wanted to play with.

Mum's boss taught Michelle to ride her bike on the aerodrome's runway. It was never very busy and gave her a good long road to ride up and down. Only the occasional executive planes and training places used to use the aerodrome.

Years later Mum helped to make a mattress for Tom Cruise's private jet. When she told me, I said "Ohhhh Mum, you could have let me have a little lie on it before you gave it back"! (What a claim to fame that would have been)..

During my first or second summer holiday I fell out of the high chair and I knocked myself out. Our neighbour Stewart rushed Mum and I to Edgeware hospital. I was so small that the nurse didn't believe I was seven. She said Mum was hysterical, only when Dad got there and confirmed my age and had Cerebral Palsy that I was seen to. I had to stay in overnight, this was the first time I had ever said a word as clear as day. I said HOME!! Mum and Dad couldn't believe it. Apparently I said it three times!

Mum often jokingly says "Maybe you should get knocked out or have a stiff drink every day so you get very relaxed, and maybe you'd be able to talk more often". I just laugh...

Possum type-writer.

About a year after going to Craig -y- Parc Miss Magor started teaching me to "write"with the use of the Possum type-writer, she had the sense to make me use my feet and I got on really well. This was when I first could show the teachers what they were saying in class was being retained, and Mum wasn't just saying I had a brain because she was the devoted mother, who just wanted to believe it.

Although it wasn't until I actually typed a letter for home that Mum really realised the extent of my intelligence. I didn't realise this until I was 45!!

I will try to describe the Possum type-writer to give you an idea of what it was and how my life was really opened up through this one piece of equipment.

The Possum type-writer had to sit on a big trolley with two shelves, which was about two foot square.

On the bottom shelf was a big clear Perspex box with loads of electric gubbins in, with sockets to put switches in.

On the top shelf had a typewriter and a big Perspex box standing vertically above the typewriter.

The vertical box had a grid of the alphabet, numbers and punctuation.

Behind each square on the grid was a light.

Miss Magor plugged two foot controls into the bottom box and put them by my feet. I would think she would have been watching my abilities for weeks and decided to give my feet a test. I took to the switches like a duck to water! I probably just typed my name on that day but it was the beginning of a love of writing for me.

I typed a letter to Mum and Dad over a few weeks as I was extremely slow at typing in those days. Thank Goodness home computers were invented and my word prediction program is a Godsend.

Mrs James taught RE and geography. I don't know if Craig -y- Parc followed the national curriculum, all that I know of but we did projects, which I enjoyed. I remember doing a project about Australia and I was amazed at the animals they have. I remember thinking the Possum was a funny name for an animal. The duck-billed platypus looked funny to me, but my favourite marsupial was the koala.

I must have told my uncle Peter that I liked koalas because he bought me a soft toy koala when I went home.

I thought I would like to go to Australia when I grew up, I didn't think it would be to see my sister Sharon in 1990.

The only RE project that I remember studying The Lord's Prayer. I think I enjoyed this project too. I am not sure that I believe in God as He is portrayed in the Bible, I believe that there has to be force that is watching us and "it" is not happy with what man is doing to the earth. I believe that Mother Nature is the force that determines everything.

Obviously this has taken me years to form this opinion and I am open to other theories.

I always loved history and learning how people lived. One of the trips we had was to St Fagan's, Wales's national museum...

It was my first outing with school, I felt really grown up going out with school mates and the teachers. I think I had just got my first wheelchair too and so I could see everything a lot easier than in a pushchair.

School friends.

Before going to Craig -y- Parc, Debbie was at a school called White Lodge, in Surrey and so there were a few other children from her primary school in the PETO unit.

My first or second "boyfriend" there was called Rory Turner, he was Debbie's friend and we kept being friends all through school.

There was a little rascal called Richard Dutton from Hereford who l liked, he was always getting told off for being naughty. He was sweet though, he left Craig y Parc about two years after l went there and l think he went to an able-bodied school at his home. I often wonder what happened to Richard, I expect he got married...

Christmas.

We would have a Christmas party with a visit from Santa. I loved it when Santa came in. Every child would get a present and a selection box of chocolate bars. I don't know where the money for around 60 presents and loads of party food came from but the staff always put on a good spread.

Just like any school, we'd put on a nativity play. The children who could talk would practice for weeks getting their parts right. Obviously us non-verbal kids couldn't have major roles in them, but we were given "silent" parts.

I must have been 8, and being very small for my age, I was quite angelic looking. I was an Angel in one year's nativity. The teachers couldn't find a halo to fit me, so they decided to put a bit of tinsel around my head for the actual performance.

The play was going really well, everyone remembered his or her lines and even Rory Turner remembered his song,

"What can I give him, Poor as I am."

Then came the last scene, where everyone gathers round the manger, of course the little ones sat at front.... I can't keep my head still at the best of times, let alone when I am excited. I hadn't seen my Mummy, Daddy or sisters for about six weeks so I was frantically looking for them in the audience.

My halo started falling down over my eyes, and the audience started going

"Ahh, look at that little girl..."

Mum and Dad must have been really embarrassed and cracking up at me. Mrs. Kerslake told one of the staff to lift my tinsel up. A hand appeared from behind the curtain and my halo was put back up to its rightful position. You could say I stole the show!!!!

Mum often teases me about that even now, and when I tell friends about this, they say,

"Mmm, that figures Nicki; sure it wasn't a sign of things to come"!

Well, maybe..

After the nativity play we all went home for Christmas holidays. I loved the Christmas holidays because I saw all my family and it was my birthday on 27th December.

We went back to school around January 7/8th every winter term. Sometimes it would snow and we would get stuck and have to turn back to go home. I remember one time getting as far as Whitchurch, about 5 miles from Pentyrch and having to turn around and go home again! I was really happy because I didn't like leaving Mum and Dad, but Dad wasn't very happy because he had to drive back to home, and do the same journey the next week.

Every year after Christmas, the whole school went to see a pantomime in Cardiff. We went on a big coach. Debbie and I always sat together.

One year Bernie Winters and Shnorbits, the St Bernard, were in the pantomime. I loved Shnorbits on the TV so to see him for real was so exciting!!

We also went out to a cinema once a year. I think the Young farmers or Round table put the cinema trips on. One of the years we saw film Song of the south, with the singing Uncle Remus and animated birds. I was amazed at the whole thing.

House parents.

We had "House parents" who looked after us during term time. Naturally we'd have favourite house parents who we got attached to…. Some of them would also have favourite children, who they'd pay special attention to. I was one of Kathy Edwards' favourite kids and she would feed me Weetabix in the big kitchen in the afternoon to try and put some weight on me and bring me sweets in. Sometimes she would take me home with her as a treat.

She also took me to my first rugby match; it was in Pentyrch and fed me Quavers all day. She must have known I would be into rugby men when I grew up!! Well not just Rugby players, I like any toned body with a brain and a good sense of humour.

I was only in the PETO group for about 2 years. I don't know why I was moved "up" to the main school, it could have been because I wasn't making enough physical progress to warrant being in the PETO group.

I can remember Mum and Dad were not happy about the decision because they could see the slight progress in me.

I was happy because I thought I was going to be with the big children. Debbie moved up at the same time and we were put in the same dormitory but different classes.

I was put into Mrs Williams' class that was just along the corridor from the PETO unit. Miss Magor helped Mrs Williams get me sitting right at my desk. I got my first wheelchair around this time. I still sat on a PETO chair in class and used the Possum typewriter. I was good with my English lessons, even though I could only type very few words a lesson.

I think Mrs Kerslake would have liked an Assembly every morning but we would usually have assemblies once a week. She was very old school and so would sing hymns and have Bible readings.

The weekdays were quite structured, with lessons and breaks ran from 9-4 and then we could do evening clubs.

Brownies and Guides.

The school had people come in the local area to do activities such as Brownies, Cubs, Scouts and Guides.

I was in the Brownies and we would have a festival in the gardens of Craig -y- Parc every year. There seemed to be lots of people there because local packs came to the school. I can't remember much about what I did at Brownies but I know I enjoyed it.

When I was about 11, I went on to be in the Girl Guides and did quite a few badges. For my service badge I did a sponsored roll on the floor. I took my sponsor form home to get people to sponsor me, I wasn't expected to do many rolls but I think I did about 20 rolls. I don't know who it was but somebody sponsored me £1 a roll, which was a lot of money in those days. All in all I raised a lot of money for the school, and it was the first of many sponsored things I have done through the years.

For my communication badge I learnt Morse code. The Guide leader wrote the Morse code out on a big piece of paper and put it up on the wall above my bed so I could see it easily. I turned my head to the left for dots, and for the dashes I looked to the right.

Morse code was would have been a good form of communication if everybody else knew it.

I took the wall chart home for the half term so that I could learn Morse code off by heart for the badge.

One day I had an itchy head and I couldn't get it across to Mum to look in my hair. In the end Mum put me on the floor and I did Morse code to her, it was

.. ¯ .. .. .. ¯. ¯.¯ .. ¯.. .. .¯ ... ¯ . ¯. .. ¯ ...

I think I have nits!!

I don't know how long I took to get that across to Mum but I must have worn a hole in the carpet!! I did have nits and I remember absolutely balling my eyes out because I thought I was dirty. Mum had to explain to me that they only go on clean hair.

I can only remember impressing my Dad once. That was when I learnt Morse code off by heart in my week's half term. I got the badge, and Dad even told his mates at work how quickly I had learnt it.

School Weekends.

The weekends were quite structured as well. On Saturday mornings Mr Petican showed films in the assembly hall. From what I remember the films were about North Sea oil and the steel industry, and sometimes nature. All very boring for kids but we were always quiet and learnt from the films.

In the afternoons we were allowed to play free in the hall. One of the house parents at school would open the sweet shop and we'd buy a lot of chocolate with our pocket money. Debbie would feed me as well as herself. Gosh, we got into some right states but it was great fun. Fortunately Saturday nights were bath nights.

Sometimes a house parent would organise a swimming pool session in the school. Some of the more able children learnt to swim. Unfortunately I have no buoyancy at all! I do a good impression of a stone though!

And so I had a helper to take me in the pool.

The "big girls" were allowed to play their records in the hall and as Cliff Richards was in his heyday that was virtually all they'd play. I am not a Cliff Richard fan needless to say. Although I admire his longevity.

On most Sunday mornings the local vicar came up to the school to do a church service. I enjoyed the Harvest service the best.

In the afternoon Trainee vicars from Cardiff theoretical college came in to do games or take us for walks or whatever we wanted to do. I can't remember how many people came but I liked Richard. All I remember is I watched The Adams family sitting on his lap.

One Sunday a group of us children went to the theoretical college. Richard pushed me around and picked me up and carried me most of the day.

I hope he became a clergyman and still remembers helping the children at Craig –y- Parc School.

My family would come to visit me some weekends and we would go out. We went to St Fagans museum one time and Dad carried me around the big house. He tripped on the stairs and instinctively grabbed the nearest thing to hand, which was a huge wall tapestry. We didn't fall and I think the wall tapestry remained intact! (I hope)

I remember getting upset and crying, I don't know why. Mum saw an ulcer under my tongue and got some Bonjella for me. I was always getting ulcers in my mouth, especially when my second teeth were coming through.

When I get ulcers in my mouth they are made worse because of my tongue thrusts.

Sports days.

I liked the spring/summer term the best because Mrs Kerslake, the headmistress, had to put on money raising events such as Garden parties in May or June. The parents and guardians would be invited to these events and of course the pupils would look forward to them.

At the end of the summer term we would have a Sport day. We would practice for a few weeks before and I liked being outside when it was good weather. The sport days were held on the big lawn if the weather was good, or in the assembly hall when the weather wasn't good.

All of the pupils took part in the sports days in whichever way they could. There were self-propelled wheelchair races, self-propelled wheelchair slaloms, beanbag throwing at a target and some running races. The pupils who couldn't do anything also took part in wheelchair races but the house parents pushed them.

Kathy Edwards always pushed me in my races and we would often win! I will admit it was pretty scary having somebody run and slalom with my wheelchair but I never came to any harm.

The sports days were held at the end of the summer term and so the parents came to them, and we would go home at the end.

I am lucky because I always went home at holiday time. However, there were some children who couldn't go home...

There was a little girl called Angela Wales who had curly ginger hair and was pretty. She had Cerebral Palsy but could talk fairly well, and she had use of one hand, and a giggle that brightened the day up.

That was all she had in the world. Her parents dumped her at CYP, she had no clothes and the house parents had to dress her in spare clothes that the school kept. She always came back from her rare visits home needing a bath and hair-wash.

Angela and I went through school together and then went to The Princess Marina Centre where we lived our young adulthood

Music.

Being like all kids, Debbie and I loved music. When The Osmonds hit the charts, in 1974, we thought they were great and Donny soon became our idol. Our parents would send us comics with pictures of them in and we would watch Top of the Pops every Thursday evening, just in case The Osmonds were on.

That summer holiday they came over to England and did a programme at the ATV studios in Elstree/Borehamwood.

Both Debbie's and my parents have always treated us as normal as possible.

Living in Borehamwood meant that the studios were literally up the road from our house and so Mum took me to see the Osmonds.. The people at the studios had all us teenyboppers on a bit of string because one minute they said that the Osmonds would be coming out of one entrance, So we'd all rush around there and cause chaos in Borehamwood high street, and then about a hour later they said that The Osmonds would be coming out of the first entrance! This went on for something like six hours. They finally appeared on top of a lorry at six o'clock and just waved. It was worth the wait... I don't think that Mum agreed.

When we went back to school, I told Debbie that not only had I seen The Osmonds, but I had met them, that I had kissed all of them, and I think I told her that Donny had sang Puppy Love to me...She didn't find out that this was a slight exaggeration for a good ten years! We still laugh about my slight exaggeration.

Speech Therapy.

I always had speech therapy all through my childhood. I can't talk or control my mouth at all, so my speech therapy was more finding the best ways to communicate and working on getting my eating and drinking manageable.

Having said that though I can get a few words out if I am relaxed and happy.. Or I am drunk I get verbal diarrhoea but more of that later.

I don't remember anything about my speech therapy when I was at Cheyne walk, but at Craig -y- Parc the head speech therapist was a lovely lady called Mrs Ena Davis. She became a special person to me, for many years...

She was a very patient lady, and would treat me every day after I had come out of the PETO unit.

I can't make a long sound with my voice if I think about it. Mrs Davis worked on improving my voice and breathing control with the help of a sound activated monkey (SAM) that climbed a plastic tree. I remember trying my hardest to get the monkey as high as possible but I only managed to get it a little way up the tree.

Having said that I can't hold a long sound intentionally, I like singing along to songs when I hear something I like on the radio or CD. Especially when I am doing my writing or painting. Often my carers ask, "Are you OK Nicki"? I spell out.. YES THANKS, I AM SINGING.. And then laugh, as sometimes they aren't exactly sure what to say!!

I have mentioned that my eating is really difficult. Mrs Davis worked a lot to get my eating better.

We went to the dentist hospital regularly for check ups. To try and get my chewing reflex working Ena thought a braise would encourage it.

Ena knew an orthodontist at the Wales university hospital in Neath.

When something is put in the side of my mouth it stimulates the chewing action, so Ena and Mr Shaw designed a braise that had two metal prongs which lightly pressed against my gums, just above the canine teeth. It worked well but I found it really uncomfortable and I didn't like the braise, and I think Ena knew it would be difficult for my future carers to put it into my mouth so we didn't pursue with the braise.

I have great difficulties with my drinking as I have said before, but Ena had the patience and skill to get me drinking through a straw. She would gently hold my chin up and close my lips around the straw so it made my sucking reflex work properly. I remember being so surprised and happy when I actually got some liquid up the straw and I swallowed properly.

Ena took some film of me eating, drinking and communicating. I don't remember why but the film was shown in India and I became pen friends with a little girl called Molly who had Cerebral Palsy too. I think Ena met Molly and her mother at a conference and got talking about me. I kept in touch with Molly for sometime after.

I don't know how long Ena had been a speech therapist at that time but she could understand my verbal sounds, and sometimes we would just chat for the whole speech therapy and often she would get Debbie to come in with me. I loved my speech therapy sessions with Ena Davis.

Ena Davis was always looking for new communication methods for the school's non-verbal children. She heard about a communication system called Blissymbolics.

Blissymbolics is a communication system originally developed by Charles K. Bliss (1897-1985) for the purpose of international communication. Blissymbolics is a language currently composed of over 2,000 graphic symbols.

It was first applied to the communication of children with physical disabilities by an interdisciplinary team at the Ontario Crippled Children's Centre (now the Bloorview MacMillan Centre) in 1971.

Ena knew that Bliss symbols would be a very good communication system for a lot of children at Craig –y- Parc.

She went to an Isaac conference in Canada. ISAAC stands for International Society for Augmentative and Alternative Communication. I remember thinking Ena must have been a very important speech therapist to go to Canada.

I was happy when she came back though and she brought me back some Maple leaf shaped fudge! Yumm!! I don't know why I remember that!!

Ena taught a few of the children how to use Blissymbols and I was put in the Bliss group.

I was able to read well, so I found Bliss symbols a little bit simple and restrictive for me.

The written word was under the symbols and so I looked for the written word. Ena soon caught on and decided I didn't need Bliss to communicate.

I think I went to the library when my class had Bliss lessons.

School friends

In 1975 Debbie left Craig y Parc when we were 11 and a half, (there's 4 months between us, I'm the eldest) and went to Thomas de la Rue school, which in those days was the grammar school of the Spastic Society (now Scope). I was upset that Debbie was leaving but knew she would be better off going to Kent. The last night of the summer term 1 can remember crying my eyes out because she was leaving.

But that was the beginning of our friendship and having that bond that would last a life time.

Home life.

I liked the summer holidays. I loved sitting in our paddling pool splashing Sharon and Michelle by kicking my legs.

The summer of 1976 was the hottest I can remember of my childhood anyway. I remember being in the garden with Dad, Sharon and Michelle one day when the ice cream van came around. Obviously Sharon and Michelle asked Dad for an ice cream and I think he got me a 99 too. Mum had gone out somewhere so Dad had to feed me. I think this was the only time Dad fed me, I can't think of another occasion.

I wasn't aware that Dad was having periods of depression. I just knew I could never get close to him.

Mum and Dad always included me on family outings. We visited all the usual places.

I remember going up to visit The Tower of London. I think Dad carried me around for a while but when we cross the bridge to the tower he had a funny feeling and just couldn't go across and almost fainted. Mum took us girls around the tower.

I remember seeing The Crown jewels sparkling in a lit glass case. I think I was about eleven and they looked so magical to me. I also remember looking at the Tower's big tarots and traitor's gate, never imagining I would write a story featuring it for my Duke of Edinburgh's Award many years later.

Mum and Dad always treated me exactly the same as my sisters... Or as near as possible...
I had a go-cart when they had bicycles....

Sharon would push me about in my go-cart; Michelle and our dog would be running in front of us. I had many scraped toes, where I'd go out in my go-cart with no socks or shoes on and my feet would drop off of the pedals. Sharon wouldn't notice my feet and carry on pushing, until I'd yell, then she'd stop... My toes would end up in ribbons!!!

When roller boots came out first, obviously Sharon and Michelle got a pair. I used to like watching them play on them... And I'd laugh when they fell over!!

One day Mum said she'd got a little present for me, and gave me a heavy box... Mum helped me to open the box. I think I laughed when I saw what was in the box! It was a pair of black and orange roller boots!!! Mum put them on me and stood me up and off we went... This was a sight to behold, Mum, Sharon and Michelle would stand me up, and my legs would just go sideways.... We'd all end up in a crumpled mess on the pavement!!! The neighbours would just laugh with us, knowing that I was doing what any kid would do.

The social workers had a fit at the things we would do, as they seem to think disabled children should be mollycoddled.

I had a friend at home called Tracy Prigmoor who also lived in Lexington Close, we were around the same age and she liked to take me for walks. I remember getting into a right old strop one evening because she had said she would come round to take me out for a walk but she didn't come. I hadn't been let down before and I learnt that sometimes people can't keep promises through no fault of their own. Tracy did come round the day after to apologise and took me out for a walk.

We would sometimes call in to see Tracy's Mum, Dad and Brother Steve.

I am a Chelsea supporter and Tracy's Dad supports Arsenal, so he would tease me. Tracy liked David Cassidy and sent me some posters of him and Donny Osmond when I went back to school.

They are a really nice family and I still see Tracy sometimes in Borehamwood as she works in HSBC, if there isn't a queue she comes out from the booth to say Hello and give me a kiss.

My first memory of Granddad's home was in a high rise flat in Cricklewood, London. I remember he had a huge gramophone in the sitting room, along with lots of African ornaments from his time in Lagos.

I think I was about ten or eleven when Granddad moved to Spur Road in Edgeware and got a bearded Collie called Bluie. He always wore a shirt and tie, a checker hat and polished shoes when he went for walks with his dog. He met a lady called Jean and they courted for a while, leading to marriage.

In about 1974 my Granddad got remarried. His wife had lots of middle names, I can't remember what they all were. When the registrar asked Granddad if he would "take Jean, something, something, something to be your wife"? Granddad got muddled up when he had to repeat all of Jean's names. This amused me immensely and I laughed out loud!

We were very close to Mum's aunty Margaret (called Queene) and Roy, and their children, Mark, Julie, Simon and Andrew. We would often go to see them as they lived in Hockley near Southend and it would take about two hours to get there because we would have to go through northeast

London. On the way we would see a tall white thing that looked like a giant Onion... I would always shout "ONION!" When I saw it. It could be miles away, but I'd always see it first and get excited!! I don't know why I was fascinated by this thing!

Roy had a yacht on the river Crouch. Roy would take us for a yacht sail and the only place he could secure me was in the front of the yacht packed out with cushions and tied to the yacht with rope. I would have a lot of fun with Sharon, Michelle, Andrew, Julie, Simon, Roy and Dad.

Mum didn't like boats and so she would see us off and go back with Aunty Margaret to her bungalow and prepare a lovely roast dinner.

After dinner Julie and I would often go into her bedroom and play records and play with dollies. I remember I liked the song "These boots were made for walking ", so Julie would always play it for me.

I always loved going to see Aunty Margaret and Uncle Roy and my cousins because I was just Nicki, who liked doing everything with everyone. I am still close to Mark, Julie, Simon and Andrew.

Mum and Dad didn't have much money to spare so we'd usually go camping in Devon with a big crowd of friends. Mum and Dad had a big circle of friends from all over North London and most of them had kids our age. We would find a big field somewhere near Barnsple with a river running through it and put up tents. There would be no facilities for camping whatsoever in the field, just running water!!

We would have a fantastic time just making a campfire and collecting wood. Every year the men would buy a whole pig or sheep and build a spit to roast the meat on, which took hours to roast. The kids never ever got burnt because we would be told not to go near the fire in no uncertain terms, but there was always an adult by the fire.

One of the gentlest, kindest, loveliest people I ever knew was Dad's friend Dennis. He didn't have children but had a dog called Miles that went everywhere with Dennis. He was great with us kids and would make a rope swing so the others could swing over the river. I would sit and watch them swing and laugh when they fell in. The men would obviously have as much fun as the kids.

The river wasn't that deep where we were camped, so when Dennis wanted to get away from us kids he would take his fold up stall and go and sit in the middle of the river, reading a book, Miles on the bank watching Dennis.

I remember Dennis playing Ian Dury tapes and telling me that he had polio.

Sadly we lost contact with Dennis sometime ago and unfortunately heard that he passed away in the 00's... I like Ian Dury records and always smile and think of Dennis when I hear him.

In September 1975 the family had a holiday at Pontings on the Isle of Wigh. This meant Sharon, Michelle and I had permission for an extra week off school. Us three girls thought it was great going on the ferry across the Solent to the Isle of Wight. I can't remember if we thought we were going abroad, but we liked Pontings a lot. We were 11, 8 and 6 respectively.

Sharon and Michelle went into the fancy dress competitions and I enjoyed watching them. Thinking about it now, Dad wouldn't have liked the entertainment as it was pretty poor and very holiday campy. The red (or blue) coats put on the entertainment.

Schoolfriends.

Dad and Mum took me back to school from the Isle of Wight and I settled in quite well, I missed Debbie a lot but I soon made a new friend called Kim Gunston. She could talk and we got on well and she became my good friend at school. She had not been to boarding school before and often would be home sick, and I would try to comfort her.

A new boy called Carlton Young started at the same time as Kim and I thought he was quite cute; in fact it was love at first sight!!! He had light brown longish hair, brown eyes and a cheeky smile. He was about a year older than me, he couldn't walk and used a manual wheelchair to get around and so had quite developed shoulders... I have got a definite liking for muscular shoulders and pecs on men, as I have got older!

Carlton and I became girlfriend and boyfriend for quite a long time and he was lovely to me. We were not in the same class but we did some clubs together.

We liked music and so went to the record club that was run in the common room, which was in the basement. The staff would help the children who could walk down the stairs first, and carry the children who couldn't walk like me.

I would always get helped to stand up to dance with Carlton and believe it or not Kathy Edwards would hold my lips together so we could have a kiss.

Family Life.

While we were on holiday in the Isle of Wight, my Uncle Peter had a fatal car crash in Totteridge, Barnet, and North London. I have learnt since then that Peter was high on drugs and just took a bend wrong and I think his mini went under a bus.

He left a young wife, Gill, and two little boys, Mark aged 4, and Tim aged 2/3.

Nanny Conway, Mum and Dad were devastated. I can't remember if Uncle Dick was around then.

Peter had just given me my koala before he died and he had given me a little girl ornament that summer holiday.

When I got home for the autumn half term Mum took me up to my bedroom and broke the news gently to me.

I was heartbroken. It was the first death that I had experienced of somebody I was close to and loved. I can remember crying a lot for a long time.

I have kept and cherish the koala and little girl ornament from Peter. They are very precious to me.

Great Uncle Harold was diagnosed with cancer in August of 1976. He died in the October.

I went back to school at the end of half term and told Kim and Carlton about Uncle Peter and Uncle Harold.

Mum and Ingrid inherited his estate in equal amounts from Uncle Harold. He also put £1000 in trust for each of their children until we were 18.

Ingrid and her family went to Disney World with their inheritance and remained in a council house.

Mum and Dad put the inheritance toward a four bed roomed house in Anthony Road, Borehamwood. The garden was about 100ft long and about 50ft wide. Dad built another huge pond, much to the annoyance of Mum.

Also Mum and Dad let granddad have a vegetable patch at the end, which he absolutely loved. Us girls loved it when granddad had the vegetable patch because he was a lovely cuddly man, and always bought us a bag of sweets. Sharon loved Curlywurlies so there was always one in the bag. I liked flakes, and still do! Michelle liked the sherbet flying saucers, yuck. I don't know how she ate them!

The house had a garage at the side, which the social worker got made into a bedroom for me. It seemed to just happen when I was a kid, there didn't seem to be all the bureaucracy about funding for anything I needed.

Dad built another garage on the other side of the house.

The house had a roof conversion, which Sharon had for her bedroom. We spent many hours up there playing...

Sharon had a dolly that was just a bust so that you could make her up. She also had an extra bit of hair that if you pulled it she could have long hair. I am not sure how you wound it back in, I think Sharon ended up cutting the long hair off.

School Life

I was always little and so the house parents would often pick me up and carry me around or help me walk. I have no speech but I can be cheeky and people who get to know me can tell when I'm being cheeky or having them on.

The school had a laundry and every night a house parent would come around all of the dormitories collecting the dirty clothes in a big bin.

I liked it when Kathy Edwards was on because she would always understand me and play about with me. If she was on laundry duty and saw me and if I'd been cheeky to her sometime, she would often get me out of my wheelchair and put me in the laundry bin.

These bins were about a metre deep and I would disappear from view! She would then wheel it around the other dormitories and ask people if they had seen me. All the time I would be giggling and shouting to get out. It was all done for fun!!

Aged eleven, I changed classes and went into Mrs Smart's class. I loved it in this classroom because it was in the old part. This classroom was probably the stables originally, as it was away from the mansion, and it was only adjoined to the mansion by a roof. There was a little road leading up to this classroom which was next to the kitchen. The majority of my school week was probably spent writing letters home, because I was so slow at typing. The whole class would write letters on Wednesday or Thursday, and so on Friday lunchtime Mrs Smart would take one of us to the post box at the end of the little road to send our letters home.

On one side of the road was a huge field, which often had sheep grazing in. I loved Mrs Smart taking me to post the letters because she get me out of my wheelchair, stand me up and watch the lambs for a few minutes, in the spring term, on the way to the post box.

Around this time, I didn't have a good time with Miss Chiltern, the physiotherapist. She was horrible to me and I don't know why. She was always telling me off, for what I don't know. She tried to make me wear a body shell. I am not sure how to describe this thing to you, but it was made from hard foam, moulded to my back. She would strap this thing on to my back and sit me in my wheelchair without securing me in.

I am floppy and I think she thought the back shell would make me sit up. Consequently I didn't feel safe and that upset me. I remember crying every time I had physiotherapy. It was bordering on abuse although I didn't realize it then. Eventually I told Kim and she rang Mum for me. I think Kim had seen her telling me off once and asked me if I wanted to ring Mum.

Mum came down to Craig -y- Parc and saw Miss Chiltern. It was decided that I would use the back shell but I would be strapped in my chair. I can't remember if Miss Chiltern continued to put the back shell on me.

I had quite a lot of physiotherapy at this time, I think Miss Chiltern gave me to the junior physiotherapist as a lost cause, but I got on better with the junior physiotherapist as she made the treatment fun.

A lot of disabled children are encouraged to horse riding because it's beneficial physiotherapy,

The Association was founded in 1965 as the Advisory Council on Riding for the Disabled with 9 Member Groups and became Riding for the Disabled Association in 1969 when membership had grown to 80 member groups. The president at that time was Lavinia, Duchess of Norfolk with HRH The Princess Anne as Patron.

I went through a stage of liking horses and went horse riding in a group from school. I think I enjoyed it in the warm weather but I gave it up when the winter came. My horse craze didn't last long.

Home Life.

Queen Elizabeth II celebrated her Silver Jubilee in 1977. The only things I remember was going to a Street party at Coniston Close, Whetstone, North London, and running in an egg and spoon race with Mum. And having a professional photograph taken with Sharon and Michelle. We wore different coloured jumpsuits which had huge collars. We were so fashionable! I liked wearing jumpsuits, although it was pretty difficult putting them on me.

I remember the big news of Elvis' death in August 1977. I knew that Mum liked Elvis' songs and she preferred him when he was young and handsome! I wasn't really aware of the effect of this death upon the world. All I remember was they had Elvis' films on TV every day during that summer holiday. I thought it was very boring. But now I like his voice. I certainly didn't realise how many singers he influenced and continues to inspire young singers.

School life.

When we went back to school Carlton Young and I split because he always played with Annette Davis. She had long blonde hair and could talk. I don't know how but she persuaded me that we didn't really need boyfriends, and so I split from my sweetheart. A few days later Annette and Carlton started going out together!! How gullible was I?

Carlton was quite able and so he left CYP the year before me and went to Thomas de la Rue. I seem to remember being in the same class as him for a little while.

I remember telling Carlton before he left that I still liked him and if he didn't have a girlfriend at Thomas de la Rue I wanted him back.

Aged 13 and a half I went into Mr Petican's class which was the senior class. I liked Mr Petican because he was a little old man who liked making things and he often invented things for the children. He was the woodwork teacher and he ran the photography club.

I was getting on great with my Possum typewriter and I was doing a lot of extracurricular activities at this time.

The senior class block had a lawn and some trees at the back of it. Mr Petican made some bird tables and put them on the lawn outside the classroom. We did a project about birds and studied their feeding habits. I really enjoy anything to do with nature and ornithology became a lifelong hobby.

Craig -y- Parc wanted to start GCSE's and I was a good candidate to do them. But all my friends were changing schools. Debbie and Carlton had already gone to Thomas de la Rue school, and Kim was going there too in the September of 1978, and so I wanted to go to this big school in Kent with Kim... I told Mum and probably Ena this and arrangements were made for me to go for an interview at Thomas de la Rue School.

I went for my interview at Thomas de la Rue School in the spring half term from Craig –y- Parc. Mum didn't like Thomas de la Rue because it was just a "normal" school building and not homely at all. I think I liked it because it was a modern building and seemed to have all new equipment… I also saw some nice boys there and so I was very keen on going there in the September.

I think I had my first migraine that day, because I was pretty nervous and excited, I was going to the new school where Debbie and Carlton were.

I went back to Craig –y- Parc for the last term and had a last night disco. There was a new housemother who got some disco lights for the school and so it was like a real "disco"!!

I liked Darts, because they were fun group. I still like their song "The boy from New York City".

I was sad to leave Craig –y- Parc school and all of the housemothers, teachers and of course Mrs Davis. But I was going on to another stage of my life and so I put a brave face on and said goodbye. I most probably had a few tears as Mum, Dad, Sharon, Michelle and I drove away.

5.

Thomas de la Rue School.

Introduction.

My spasms get worse when I am worried or nervous and although I was looking forward to going to Thomas de la Rue I was pretty nervous, so Mum asked our GP if she could give me something to calm them down. I think he put me on Mogadon, but I didn't take them for long.

We got our first cat that summer holiday. We called her Tiger. She was so poorly and had mites in her ears and half a tail!! She must have cost Mum and Dad an absolute fortune in vet's fees but she turned out to be a lovely affectionate cat ever!!

She was tiny and could sleep on my bum if I went on my tummy on the floor. My bum was tiny too, so she must have been very small!! I have a lovely black and white photo of Tiger on my bum...

She grew into a fat and fluffy cat. She loved to be carried around on Mum's hip and also used to kiss Mum. When we had boxes of Maltesers in the house, Tiger would sneakily put a paw in the box, hook one out and bat it around the house! It was so funny.

I wasn't into the punk scene, and I don't think I was really aware of what punk was then. However I liked some of the music that got into the charts. I remember liking the Blondie song Denis because it was fresh and her voice was really different. I also liked the Genesis, "Follow you follow me" with Phil Collins on lead vocals.

Sharon had a friend called Linda Simpson who had an elder brother, Kevin, and a big sister called Kim.

The Simpsons lived between Radlett and Borehamwood, on Theobald Street. They lived in one of the three cottages with a long garden with fields all around. In those days it was safe to play in the surrounding countryside that the Organ Hall cottages back onto.

Linda's sister was about 17 and was training to be a care assistant and so Mum asked Kim to look after us sometimes. I liked Kim looking after us because we went to all the playgrounds in Borehamwood and she would get me out of my wheelchair and take me on the swings or threadle me into a baby swing so I could feel as if I was doing it myself. Or we'd go to see her parents, Pete and Brenda, and have lunch there. They are really lovely people and always treated me like anyone else, I don't know if they had had contact with a severely disabled person before but I never felt different from my sisters in their house.

I liked Kim's brother, Kevin, a lot. I think he was a few years older than me. I remember Kevin made me laugh and was nice to us.

New School.

In the September of 1978, aged 14, I started at Thomas De la Rue school, Tonbridge, Kent.

The school was set on fire in the summer holiday so about half the school was shut off and we had a few port-a-cabins for rooms. I can't remember what rooms were lost in the fire but the physiotherapy gym was a makeshift dining room, and the physiotherapy gym was in a port-a-cabin. There were two separate buildings which were the dormitory blocks. Obviously we were all teenagers and so the hormones were running riot.

Over the next two years the school was rebuilt with little disruption to school life.

In my first year I was in a dormitory with four girls. I can't remember exactly who they were but we all had Cerebral Palsy and after a few days got on well together.

Our houseparent was a lady called Jane. I liked Jane because she treated all her girls as adults and dealt with the inevitable tears and moody, teenage girls in her stride.

The school had changed from being the grammar school of the Spastic Society, into being the comprehensive school and I was put in the low achievers class.

This was really frustrating. For a start, I could read, which the others couldn't do.

I was mucked around something chronic at this school. I had been using the possum with my feet and was getting on well with it. Almost as soon as I started there, the occupational and physiotherapist therapists decided to stop me using my foot controlled possum typewriter and made me use an ordinary typewriter with a head attachment. This was ridiculous as I didn't (never did) have very good head control and could not press the correct letters on the keyboard. They also got me a Brother type-writer which was one of the smallest type-writers you could get. I had no chance of doing any proper school work, let alone doing my GCEs.

The physiotherapist and occupational therapist said it was not socially acceptable to use your feet to do things, albeit a lot of people with Cerebral Palsy automatically use their feet from little.

I don't know why the therapists thought it was not "socially acceptable" to use your feet, or whatever you could use most effectively. This was totally different from Craig –y- Parc's view and has always baffled me.

Then, oddly, the Physio therapist decided to get me a foot controlled electric wheelchair, which was great but they also thought I'd be better controlled if my arms were tied down to the wheelchair. So I got a huge wheelchair with loads of cushions to fit me and horrendous black arm gutters on with straps on. The idea of doing this was to stop my arms flying about and make me control my head better.

At first I think I quite liked having my left arm secured, because it did help a little bit, but it soon started to have more of a negative effect because my spasms became worse, and subsequently started my back twisting..

The physiotherapist were not thinking about my future health and bodily mobility, they just thought if I was fixed in one position it was immediately better for me and my carers.

I still use a foot controlled electric wheelchair, but the horrendous arm gutters went as soon as I left school, Mum discovered a better way of safely securing my arms..

The school day was split up into lesson periods and we would have different teachers for separate subjects. For most lessons the teachers would come to us because we needed our own type-writers and lugging books around would have been a nightmare. For subjects like art, home economics, the therapies, woodwork and PE we would go to the respective room.

A few of the classroom assistants twigged that I could do a lot more educationally and they would sometimes take me to the library and read the age appropriate with me. I was really miserable because it was so frustrating and I knew that I could do a lot more.

In the four years 1 was there 1 had three really good teachers, who were able to see beyond my physical disability.

The main one, Tim Rogers, the maths and general studies teacher. I loved his lessons because he saw my eyes and knew I wanted to learn. I also thought he quite good looking and had a gentle nature about him

I liked the art class a lot and got on really well with the teacher Mrs Boyce. Not long after I had been using it, Mrs Boyce started attaching crayons to my head attachment and I slowly began to do squiggles. I think eventually I drew a sort of impression of a Yorkshire terrier, which lead her to tell me about the Impressionists.

She decided to do a class project about the impressionists, which ended with a trip to The National Gallery in London. It was my first visit to a gallery and I remember being in awe of all the paintings!

During the lessons I particularly liked Renoir's work. I liked his "Umbrellas" the best and it was amazing to see the full size painting in reality.

I have continued to study the impressionists and although I like Monet and Van Gough I think Renoir is my favourite.

Down the corridor from the art room was the typing classroom, that had about 10/12 type-writers in.

I got on well with Mrs McKaskill, the typing teacher, because she was always pleased to see me and would spend most of the lesson trying to get me typing easier. She must have also been so frustrated because she knew that I could be doing much more educationally if I was using my feet to type.

She had seen me using my Possum type-writer before it was taken away from me.

I remember going to the typing room every day and trying desperately to type better and quicker with my head attachment, but it was no good, I just didn't have that good head control and I'd get upset with frustration. I would spend the whole lesson trying to copy the "Grease" lyrics out for typing practice, only managing to type a few words at a time. I went right off of that film for years!!

I also quite enjoyed the science lessons because the teacher was nice to me, although his teaching left a lot to be desired. Mr Arthur lived in one of the houses in the school grounds and so he was around a lot. Mr Arthur, aka PJ, had a little boy called Nicky, who took a shine to me. He would always run up to me and babble to me. He was a cute kid and I grew quite fond of little Nicky.

There was a nice young PE teacher called Andy Gould at Thomas de la Rue School. He had dark hair and big eyes. I think he was quite short and stocky build but quite fit with it. I remember all the girls liked him, me included.

My shoes would often fall off and staff would have to put them back on for me... One day it happened when Andy Gould was passing me and so he naturally came over and put it back on for me. Obviously he chatted to me which I liked... I must have told my friends about this because ever after I kicked shoe off as he passed me, especially when the girls were around... I became quite efficient at kicking just one shoe off

83

as Andy Gould was passing close by me. I would be giggling and he must have twigged but played along with me, because it worked every time...

I should remember this trick now. But I never remember to do it.

The school had a small library where the students could go to study and play quiet board games. At one end of the library was a comfy seating area with some bean bags for us to relax in. The staff would get the severely disabled students out of their wheelchairs and put us the bean bags without any qualms about health and safety issues. Some of the male students were as big as men and they were still lifted out their wheelchairs and put us into floppy bean bags.

I loved the warmth and cosiness while sitting in them and often fell asleep in them.

I liked the board game Othello, it was my favourite game.

Although my class time was mostly wasted, my social time was really good, and made up for the extremely frustrating class time. The school had "prep time" after school hours, most of the teachers never set my class to do any prep so I would go to the library where there would be staff and students to talk to, and somebody would set a book up for me to read. Or take me for a walk around the school grounds.

I remember feeling left out when my piers were being trained to be independent. I longed to go to the Cooper hut with a group of girls and be "independent" like other students. The Cooper hut was a separate building which was kitted out with a wheelchair accessible kitchen and the rest of a house. I don't know, I was never allowed to go in there, even though my piers asked if they could invite me to have a cuppa and a chat.

The annoying thing was that I could see the Cooper hut from the dormitory. I have discovered as time has gone by that independence is a state of mind and not what you can physically do.

My First Holiday Abroad.

I think it was in June 79 that my family had our first holiday abroad. We flew from Luton airport to Malta for a fortnight. I remember being very excited about going in a plane for the first time. In those days airports were not really set-up for disabled travellers.

I think I was put into a huge wheelchair at the check-in so that my wheelchair could be taken to the plane's hold. I would have been flopping about like a pea in a colander because I was only the size of an 8yr old, even though I was 15!

Dad, Mum, Sharon and Michelle, Nan Conway and I checked in and every one was very excited about going on a plane.

We stayed in a self catering Apartment complex called Mascascarla in St Paul's Bay.

There was a Swimming pool in the Apartment complex which us girls and Dad loved going in. Mum doesn't like water generally but she got me a rubber ring and every day we went in the pool and gradually I got my confidence up. Eventually I could do a width on my back, on my own, obviously Mum always stayed nearby just in case I flipped over!!

We hired a car in Malta and went around the island almost every day. The Maltese have great food and we found a patisserie which made their own cottage cheese pastries, which were delicious. We would get some of them most days and they would be devoured.

The Maltese are lovely people and very kind to children. We went to a firework display, I don't remember where it was but it was in a village and was amazing. We were given sweets and orange juice by the villagers.

The holiday Apartment complex had a café around the pool and we would often go to the café for lunch or dinner. Inevitably I had my first crush on a waiter!! I think his name was Carlos or something like that. I don't remember what he looked like, probably typically Mediterranean.

We went to the capital of Valletta and went into the Cathedral. It was the first time I was aware of the Catholic requirement of women covering their shoulders and heads.

We stopped at a market one day. Mum and Dad had been told that pick pockets were rife in the markets and to be aware. Unfortunately Nan was a simple and gentle lady and just wandered around with her purse in one hand and had her purse nicked at a market. I don't remember but I expect Dad had a go at poor Nan.

I loved my first holiday abroad and started a love for travelling and seeing different countries.

Unfortunately when Mum got the photos developed, none of them came out. We don't have any photos of Malta...

Mum and Dad took me back to Thomas de la Rue and all I could think about was Malta...

School life.

In what was supposed to be my last year of school, I was put in a dormitory with Kim Gunston and Zoe Waddington. We were allowed a few privileges down in this dormitory, like we could have our own coffee and biscuits in the common room and radio on in the morning.

There was a record player and fridge in this common room and the able girls were encouraged to make the coffee and teas, while the boys would play the records and try chatting us girls up. I had a few boyfriends there although I still had this crush on Carlton Young, but he was with a girl called Debbie Ward. I had a nice boyfriend called Mike Kender and we were always going out together and then breaking up...

My mates there were Paddy Devine, I fancied him a lot but he was not interested in me, but we got on well and he would often chat to me.

One of the nicest people I have ever met was Helen Parr. She was a really nice girl, so down to earth. We sat together at meal times for most of our time at Thomas de la Rue and became good friends for quite some time. Helen was a lot more able than me, but her right arm seemed like it had a mind of it's own. Poor Helen literally did not know what it would do next. Her Cerebral Palsy was quite severe but she was quite able. She had good speech and could use her legs to propel her wheelchair. The best aspect of Helen was her sense of humour and her ability to laugh at herself.

Around 1979/80 there was a TV sci-fi series called "The day of the Triffids". It was about giant plant that took over the earth and could reach anywhere. One day Helen and I were watching this programme and she said something like "that is like my arm! I never know what my arm is about to grab"!! I remember bursting into laughter and we got chucked out of the TV room!! She referred to her arm as "Triffid" ever after...

The school's heart throb was a chap called David Bolton. He was quite able and had been at a normal school until then. He was quite good looking and often chatted to me. I didn't really know David then, as he always seemed to have a girl glued to his face. He will kill me for that but it is true...

Since social networking websites have sprung up, David and I have been in touch and are quite good friends. He is a really smashing, kind and funny person.

My favourite house mother was Chris Rich. She was a really kind and bubbly lady and every one liked her. She gave me the nickname Maggot because I was really little.

We could go into Tonbridge or Sevenoaks on a Saturday afternoon. Students like me would have to ask for a member of staff to take us on the minibus, while the more able students would get a bus or share a taxi.

I liked going into Tonbridge with Chris Rich because she would take me into the clothes shops and show me all the pretty dresses that she liked. Unfortunately I was too small for anything remotely fashionable because in those days they just didn't make fashionable clothes for little teenagers, like me. Thankfully that changed in the 1980's and I can get more or less what I like, apart from shoes.

I was still going to see the paediatrician Dr at Cheyne Walk every year. Mum and Dad always trusted his advice and suggestions for me.

I would have been 15 when Dr Foley recommended I got a walker so I could keep the strength in my legs and also my breathing benefited from any walking. Mum took me to the Naidex in Birmingham and brought me the walker Dr Foley recommended...

The Physiotherapists at Thomas de la Rue were not happy that Mum had got this walker for me. Again their philosophy was I couldn't walk properly so I should be stuck in a wheelchair for the rest of my life. Chris Rich was the only person to see that it was good for me to stand up and so she put me in it so I could have the freedom of walking. The other kids loved seeing me walking.

Music.

I have always loved listening to the radio and music in general. I remember when the novelty song "Toast" by The Q-Tips came out in '78/9. I didn't take any notice of the lead singer, just thought it was a fun song... Although I remember thinking "like his dimples and smile". (Never imagining I would ever meet him and have him recognise me in an audience 42 years after "Toast" was in the charts) I am a huge Paul Young fan and have most of his records, CDs and DVDs.

Zoe and I loved the Adam Ant LP Kings of the wild frontier, with "Ant music and Prince Charming" on. We also liked the videos because they were full of story and stars.

Another of my favourite singers at this time was Leo Sayer. Mum took me to see Leo Sayer at Hammersmith Odeon for my 15th or 16th birthday. Mum had arranged for me to go back stage and meet him. He was really nice to me and signed a LP for me. That was the start of my love of live music.

School Holidays.

That Christmas holiday was awful because Mum and Dad were arguing a lot. Dad's depression was really bad and lead to arguments between them.

New Year's Eve Mum had had enough and took us girls to stay with Nanny Conway for a few days.

One day, in July 1980 Mum came to see me at school. I thought it was a little odd because it was a mid-week day but it never occurred to me that anything drastic was wrong at home. At lunch time, I was taken to the headmaster's office where Mum and her friend were waiting for me. I remember being really happy to see Mum. She got me out of my electric wheelchair and sat me on her lap and told me that my Dad had had a car accident the day before, and had died. I remember screaming at first in total disbelief, and then I cried.

I was absolutely devastated...

Mum asked me if I wanted to go to Dad's funeral. I didn't go to Dad's funeral because I was scared of funerals. I really don't know what I was scared of and I regret not going to say goodbye to Dad properly. But Mum couldn't have coped with me and Sharon and Michelle at the funeral anyway, as she was in total shock.

Apparently there were loads of people at Dad's funeral and the road to the cemetery, Allum Lane, Borehamwood, was solid with motorbikes and cars.

I don't remember a lot about that time, but I remember how good all my friends were really good to me. They really got me through the grief...

I didn't have much to do with Debbie at that time, I don't know why, although when Dad died she was there for me.

Kim Simpson was living with Mum and Dad at the time, I'm not sure why. From what I have been told Dad was working on his car. He asked Kim to make him a cup of coffee and went back into the garage and shut both doors and then started the car up... Both of the garage doors were closed and he was overcome by fumes. Kim took the drink to Dad and found him slumped over in the car..

I found out some years later that the Coroner's report came back as death by misadventure. It meant that Dad didn't intentionally kill himself, he wanted to be found.

So it was not suicide... The difference is that it was accidental, it was not intentional... Which is a little comfort for me.

Sharon and Michelle were 13&12 respectively. I don't know how they coped at time because we don't talk about that time.

Lourdes.

The RE teacher, Mr Eastwood, had taught my class about the miracles that supposedly happen at Lourdes in the South of France. I was undecided about my religious beliefs but I was interested in the miracles happening. At this time I was still quite unaware of the bad things in life and cynicism hadn't entered my head yet.

Tours from all over the world are organized to visit the Sanctuary. Connected with this pilgrimage is often the consumption of or bathing in the Lourdes water which wells out of the Grotto.

I have absolutely no idea how it came about but the summer holiday after Dad had died, I went to Lourdes with the Across group, on the Jumblance.

I also asked Mum if she remembers how I came to go to Lourdes that year and she doesn't know either.

ACROSS/Jumbulance is a recognised charity created specifically to provide Pilgrimages by Jumbulance to the Christian Marian Shrine of Lourdes in SW France for those who are sick and disabled.

The Jumbulance is a unique vehicle with ambulance status, specially constructed to carry very sick and disabled people accompanied by volunteer able bodied nurses, doctors and helpers. Priority is given to those in terminal illness.

Mum and I met the organiser, Ian McNiff, and the Jumbulance at a church in London for the long journey through France to Lourdes in the South of France. The Jumblances had like stretcher beds along one side of it and I was laid on one for the journey, and I was allocated a helper.

This was my very first holiday on my own but I don't remember being nervous or worried about anything.

I think the journey took over a day and although I slept on the Jumblance I was pleased to get to Lourdes. The Across hotel was built like a French Chateau and very pretty.

The surrounding countryside was beautiful as it isn't far from the French Pyrenees.

I was a bit confused about my religious beliefs at this time, and was totally baffled when we had the first Mass in the across hostel. I had never been to a Catholic service.

I enjoyed the candle light walk down to the grotto where Mary appeared to Saint Marie-Bernarde Soubirous. I was also impressed when I saw the big white chapel that had been built there. I can't remember actually going into the chapel but I suppose we must have. I also remember thinking how lavishly built the chapel was for a little French village.

One day we did a walk up a hill to do the stations of The Passion, I think I enjoyed this more than anything because I love being in the open air, and although I don't practice my given religion I appreciate the time and work that had gone into creating the stations of The Passion..

It was only very shortly after Dad had died and it was a very weird but peaceful place for me to be. I remember one day I got upset about Dad. I think Ian McNiff got me out of my wheelchair and gave me a cuddle. All the helpers were really kind and took good care of me.

During the holiday a song came out by a group called Matchbox, called "When you talk about love".

It must have been on the radio in Lourdes because I remember looking at Ian and laughing. One of the lines went,

"... What you feel for me is infatuation, it all started back on summer vacation".

I always laugh when I hear that little song and think of Ian.

I think it was near the end of my holiday that the group went down to the grotto where Mary appeared to Bernadette, there is a water spring which is thought to be healing water.

I don't remember much about it but I think there were stone baths in a cave next to the grotto where the sick and disabled get submerged to be (hopefully) cured. Obviously I was dunked in the "healing water", which was absolutely bloody freezing! If I get sudden extreme temperature change I go into full spasm and that was certainly extreme temperature change! It was awful and I hated it. It didn't do me a lot of good as I caught a terrible cold.

I was glad to get home after a long journey on the Jumbluance. I said goodbye to everyone and Mum drove away for home and put me to bed.

I enjoyed the holiday. My lasting memory was the beautiful countryside, and Ian McNiff; but I found Lourdes really commercial and in some respects a bit tacky.

I bought a bottle of "holy water" back to go under Dad's headstone.

Last year at School.

In September 1980, I went back to school and some of my friends had left the previous term, but I don't remember who left as I was very upset about Dad. I think I was put into a better class educationally because I remember we read "A

Town Like Alice", which was a GCE set book the year before. I know this because I remember Kim and others studying it.

Andy Gould, the PE teacher, had left the term before and Mr Rogers became the PE teacher, which I thought was good. Although I did miss kicking my shoes off just as Andy passed me!

It had taken 2 years to rebuild the fire damaged part of the school but eventually the new building was finished. We had a new dining room, common room, toilets and a huge assembly hall. It was great to have the school as it was supposed to be.

Ian McNiff and I had been writing to each other since the Lourdes holiday and he came to see me one day in the autumn term. I remember sitting in the front entrance hall waiting for him and two of the helpers from the holiday. When I saw them coming up the path of the school toward me, I got very excited and I was beaming as they came in the door.

Ian was 21 and quite good looking, his whole humour was gentle.

They took me out for the afternoon and we had tea out.

In December John Lennon was fatally shot in New York. I remember thinking; well at least his kids are going to be OK for money, although I knew how devastated they'd be.

In the morning assembly we said a prayer for John Lennon, I got upset because it wasn't long after Dad went and he liked The Beatles.

International Year of Disabled Persons (IYDP)

The year 1981 was the International Year of Disabled Persons (IYDP) by the United Nations. It called for a plan of action with an emphasis on equalization of opportunities, rehabilitation and prevention of disabilities.

Ian Dury wrote a song, Spasticus Autisticus, in response to what many saw as a "crashingly insensitive" idea.

"Spasticus Autisticus" was written in 1981 for the International Year of Disabled Persons. It was a cross between a battle cry and an appeal for understanding. Quote: "Hello to you out there in normal land. You may not comprehend my tale or understand!"

The lyric was deliberately provocative, as the word Spastic, a name for sufferers of Cerebral Palsy, was becoming taboo in Britain, due to its use as a derogatory term.

This was silly because everyone knew what a "Spastic" was, despite of its derogatory use. I loved the song. Dennis and I listened to it together and I understood the song.

Dury was himself disabled from polio, but the BBC deemed it offensive to polite sensibilities and denied it airplay.

I don't remember this but Mum told me that Dennis was worried about playing "Spasticus Autisticus" to me because he thought I'd be offended by the lyrics.

I sometimes play this song because it is on an Ian Dury CD. As much as I don't find it offensive, I know that some people may find it offensive through not knowing original intentions, and that Ian Dury was disabled himself. But, moreover, he was a brilliant writer.

At last, the end of term came and I was leaving TDS to go home for good. I think I was a bit sad about saying goodbye to my friends and a few of the teachers and houseparents but I wanted to go home to live.

6.

Northampton. And Back to TDS.

Introduction.

This was a time of flamboyancy in the business and fashion world, after the dreary 70's in the UK. Margaret Thatcher was Prime minister. The New Romantic music genre was all the rage, and the new fashion for both sexes was heavy make-up and frilly shirts. Or sharp suits and shoulder pads.

A buzz was going around the country that Prince Charles and a young Dianna Spencer were getting married.

I remember seeing this young nursery nurse being harassed by the paparazzi and feeling sorry for her. She may have courted them sometimes but she didn't deserve the constant invasion of everything she did.

For Mum, Sharon, Michelle and I it was a time of grieving and trying to come to terms with Dad's death. I can't remember if I felt the loss as much as Mum, Sharon and Michelle because I wasn't very close to Dad.

A few months after Dad died, Mum decided to move up to Northampton to make a necessary break for us all.

Mum had two able bodied daughters who were about to become teenagers. Sharon was 13 and Michelle was 12. I can only imagine that Mum wanted to protect them and so Sharon and Michelle went to an all girls school, which neither liked.

Nan Holmes went off to Spain to live. This was another bitter blow to Mum because she really needed a mother's support in her young widowhood. Mum was only 35 when Dad died.

l was coming up to 17. I don't think that I was even given a chance to college after school. This didn't bother me at the time as I wanted to go home which Mum had always promised me I could do.

I left Thomas de la Rue School in 1981, at the same time as all of my friends. In hindsight I should have gone onto Hereward College in Coventry, to do exams and learn some life skills. Although the technology I would have needed to enable me to study had not become readily available to individuals at that time.

As it was I think I lack some knowledge about how to deal with certain situations, has lead to lots of situations I haven't been able to handle.

Sharon and Michelle and I were still children a social worker was assigned to us. Mr. King was one of the few very good social workers we have had. He had the experience and knew how to get the appropriate activities for me.

Unfortunately there were not many things for a severely disabled young woman to do in those days.

Mr King organised for me to go to a work centre, in Northampton twice a week but I hated it! It was full of elderly people and the staff had no idea what to do with a young physically disabled person.

On the other days I had a tutor come to the house to do English with me. Sometimes we went into the local school and did some painting. For some odd reason she decided I should try to paint with my feet. Although I use my feet to use my electric wheelchair and my PC switches, I can't hold anything with my toes so I don't know what on earth she was thinking of. Nevertheless it was good fun, if messy!!!!

The Grand Union canal runs through Northampton and the tutor thought it would be a good idea to do a project about canals. We went to see the canal at Stony Stratford which is about 15 miles from Northampton.

It was in the winter of 1981/2 which was a really hard winter and in those days there were no wheelchair accessible paths to the canals, so Mum and the tutor had to take me over fields and styles to get to the canal. It was absolutely freezing traipsing across the countryside!

I found it very interesting learning about the canal people's lives and I must have said I would like to write a story as the Tutor helped me write a story about canal people. I didn't finish it then but many years later I rewrote it for children, and included it in my book.

Phab Club.

Mum and I thought it would be a good idea if I could meet some people in the local area, so we asked Mr King about a Phab Club. Phab stands for physically handicapped and able bodied, and they aim to promote independence and inclusion.

It is good for kids and young adults and I quite enjoyed going to the Northampton Phab club because it got me out of the house one evening a week. But many Phab clubs also accept learning disabled people. I don't think it is good to make physical disability and learning disabilities mix as they have different needs and requirements, in every aspect of life.

I remember trying to talk to one of the Phab leaders and they just patronised me, because they didn't know how to talk to me as a knowing person. It wasn't their fault; they were not used to somebody like me.

However, I am not keen on Phab clubs because of my experiences. But I think the Phab organisation does really good work for kids with disabilities and learning disabled people.

Granddad.

Granddad had his first heart attack in the autumn of 1981, so Mum had to keep going up and down the M1 to visit him. It was about a 150 mile round trip and Mum did it nearly everyday. I remember her being really worried about granddad. He recovered quite well from this heart attack but had to lose weight. He was always a happy, chubby man before his heart attack, but after that happened he never seemed the same.

Hen.

It was my 18th in the December. I had always wanted my own dog but being away at school for much of my childhood it wouldn't have been practical. But as we thought I'd come home for good, Mum said I could have a puppy for my birthday.

We looked in newspapers for litters of puppies and saw a private breeder who had some Yorkshire Terrier puppies that had just been born, so Mum rang the breeder and reserved a little girl puppy for me.

A few weeks later we went to see the puppies for a little while as the breeder had chosen one puppy for me and had been calling her the name Mum had told her to.

As she was a pedigree dog, she had to have a kennel name. Her full name was Henrietta Flightermouse, but I decided to call her Hen.

Mum and I sat on the breeder's sofa. The puppies were with their Mum in another room. The breeder opened the door with a tiny bundle of fluff in her hands and then put it on the sofa, beside Mum. All of a sudden this little ball of fluff took a run across Mum's and my lap and leaped off the end of the sofa!! The breeder smiled at me and said "That is why I called her Flightermouse, she's always done that"!!

I was looking forward to my birthday as I was going to have an 18th birthday party... Mum booked a hall back in Edgware, North London, for me. It was the first big party we had ever had because although Mum and Dad had a lot of dinner parties we had never had anything to celebrate before. Obviously I don't remember Mum or Dad's 21st's...

I don't remember a lot about the party as it was a very long time ago now but I invited a lot of my school friends and all the family. Only Nanny Conway came from the Conways. But I was happy that Patrick Devine and Miss Brewer came. Unfortunately it was the last time I saw them

I think Miss Brewer probably knew that I had a great family and would do well in life, and she had other children to take under her wing.

And Patrick and I lost touch for many years but the internet came in useful eventually.

I was very small for my age and so Mum could put me on the floor to play with Hen. She loved running around me like a mad thing, or grabbing my sleeves and I would get my arm to drag her around me. This was OK and great fun until my hand grabbed her little leg, then Mum or Sharon and Michelle would have to rescue little Hen from my hand! I would feel awful when that happened obviously, but there was nothing I could do about it because my spasms are involuntary. She would soon come back and get my sleeve and tug my right arm again. Or she would attack my feet and pull my socks off but I could get her off of her feet and tickle her with my feet!!

I continued going to the day centre twice a week but I really was not getting any benefit from it because they didn't understand that I had an active brain and I needed more specific activities than they had to offer.

I was still struggling with the little Brother type-writer and I would type letters to my friends from school. I had also kept in touch with my favourite houseparent at Thomas de la Rue, Chris Rich. I invited her up to see me. I seem to remember we went to Northampton centre and went shopping and had lunch out. It was as much of a break for Mum as a day out for me.

Skylarks.

My social worker, Mr King, suggested that I may like to have a break and brought some information for me to long at about The Winged Fellowship Trust.

In 2004 it became Vitalise.

Vitalise have respite centres in Southampton, Cornwall, Chigwell, Southport and Nottingham.

I decided that I would like to go to Skylarks in Nottingham, as it wasn't too far away from Northampton. Mr King brought the Winged Fellowship Trust's application forms around Mum filled them in.

I can't remember what time of year I went there but it rained a lot, especially the first week.

The Skylarks holiday centre was quite near Nottingham city and I remember seeing the cricket ground and the river Trent. I have absolutely no idea why I remember seeing the cricket ground as I have absolutely no interest in the sport!

But the Skylarks centre was quite nice and modern and they had good activities laid on, and the staff were nice.

There were trips out laid on by Skylarks and I went to my first nightclub in Nottingham. I was so excited because one of the staff had heard that a new duo had just hit the charts who I really liked and they were going to be at the night club. I saw Yazoo in 1981 when they had just hit the charts with Only You and have followed the amazing Alison Moyet ever since.

I bought the tape Upstairs at Eric's the next day.

I think I must have become close to a member of staff and they could cope with my care and communication needs enough to take me camping near Chatsworth house in Derbyshire. I think we went for about four days and visited Chatsworth house one day.

I know I recognised Chatsworth house when the TV programmes "Pride and prejudice" and The Antiques Roadshow have been on. .

I soon returned home to Northampton at the end of the fortnight and got very fed-up with the limitations of being without my electric wheelchair or typewriter..

Back to Borehamwood.

None of us were happy living up in Northampton so we decided to move back down to Borehamwood. Mum found a three bed roomed house with potential to build an extension as I needed a down stairs bedroom. I was getting too lanky for Mum to carry down stairs. Although Mum could assist me to walk up stairs.

Mum bought an ex council house in Stanborough Avenue, in Borehamwood, Hertfordshire. It was basically a shell and we had to decorate the whole house. Mum also had a room built on the back of the dining room for my bedroom. From what I can remember we had quite a big garden and so my bedroom didn't take much of it up.

Sharon was in the middle of her GCEs, and she went to Nicholas Hawkesmore School on Cowley road in Borehamwood. Most of Sharon's friends were at Nicholas Hawkesmore School and I think she had a good time there. She was a very bright student and didn't work very hard for her exams but she still left school with good grades. However she went onto higher education later in life.

Mum couldn't get Sharon and Michelle into the same school and so Michelle went to Hillside School, which was supposed to be a less academic school. I don't think Michelle was too happy about this but she really knuckled down to her education and left with A Levels.

I went with Mum to the house everyday as I had nothing else to do for a few months. It was really very boring for me, even though Mum set me up making a cork fly curtain. I must have painted hundreds of bloody corks at the time and I don't know if the curtain even got made.

In those days, there were hardly any day service centres that could cope with my particular needs of daily care and intellect, so it was pointless even looking for one.

I can't remember how long it took for the house to be done enough so that we could live in it but Mum and Colin decided to live together. All of us kids were happy about this arrangement, after all, we had known Colin and Eve all our lives.

Mum informed social services that we had moved back to Borehamwood and fortunately our old Social worker was assigned to us again.

Gillian Thursby was a newly qualified social worker and very good at her job. After discussing it with Gillian and Thomas de la Rue school I decided that I would go back to school while Gillian started the ball rolling for me to go to the Princess Marina Centre in Beaconsfield, Bucks.

YDH.

Before I went back to school I went on holiday to Lancaster University, with Young Disabled on Holiday, in about the August of 1982. There were a few people from the London area so I think we met some of the organisers at Euston train station to go to Lancaster.

The helpers were all volunteers and it was a mammoth task for the organisers to get enough volunteers to run the holidays.

There seemed to a lot of people at the university and I think I was quite nervous on my first night there.

I can't remember a lot about this holiday apart from I fancied an able-bodied fellow called Trevor Lawley! He seemed like a nice guy and was quite cute with dark hair, brown eyes and a cute smile. Trevor had come on holiday with his girlfriend. They were helpers. She was a blonde, blue eyed lass called Julie and really nice to me. Trevor wore a green felt hat all week and on the last night, I think we had a dance on the last night disco and had a photo taken together. He gave me a peck on my cheek and his hat!! (& his address). I was so happy because I was given this hat, I wore it all the way home on the train!

I wrote to Trevor after the holiday but only heard from him once. I wonder if Trevor and Julie remember me..

I was glad to get home from the YDH holiday and Mum's cooking, also I was looking forward to seeing Debbie again.

Friends.

My best friend, Debbie, came to stay with us for a weekend in the summer holidays of 1982. I can't remember exactly when but it was when the Fame film was out and so we went to see it. Mum and Colin took us up to London. It was a certificate 15a film. I didn't look my age so the usher (a boy of about 18) asked how old I was, Mum said that I was 18 but he didn't believe her. He actually tried to get me out of the cinema until Mum asked to see the manager.... Anyhow we saw Fame and the usher shut-up.

The same year, a very good family friend said she was pregnant and I told Babs that I had a feeling it was going to be a girl, so we made a pact that if she had a girl I would be her daughter's Godmother.

When Mum told me that Babs had had a girl, of course I went into fits of laughter and got excited. Mum didn't have a clue what I was going on about so she rang Babs to find out. The baby became known as little Michelle, so that Mum knew who l was talking about.

Back to Thomas de la Rue.

I returned to Thomas de la Rue School in November 1982. Mum, Colin, Sharon and Michelle, and my little dog Hen, took me back. Although I was glad to go back to school to do something with my brain, and have the freedom of being able to have my electric wheelchair. I missed my family and my little dog Hen.

The new headmaster had told Gillian Thursby that they had recently got a lot of computers and I could learn how to use the apple computer which had the only communication program that was for severely disabled people to use.

I was put in the class that were studying for their GCEs and City and Guilds exams. I had a good friend called Nick Turner that had come to Thomas de la Rue from Craig –y-Parc School in the year I was at home. He was a lot more able than I am, and he liked taking me for walks around the school grounds. Sometimes the staff would organise swimming sessions. I would have a member of staff with me. Nick could swim and he would splash me and tickle my feet. He was a little rascal generally. After leaving school, Nick became a Cobbler and had his own business in Kington, Herefordshire. We lost touch for a long time after school but we found each other on Facebook and our friendship rekindled easily.

After the Christmas holidays of 1982 I had my own room in the same dormitory block that I had shared with Kim and Zoe. My room was rather small and dingy but I

111

put some posters and photos up on the wall and I had my faithful radio/casset with me. I didn't spend much time down in my dormitory block and so I spent most of my time up in Davis block with Helen Par... Davis block was a self contained unit where students had their own room, communal kitchen and lounge, and bathroom facilities. Davis block was for the 6th form as they needed somewhere to study and become independent.

I would often have my tea with Helen Parr, if a houseparent could be spared from the main dining room to feed me.

I was very small for my age and so I was about 18/19 when I started my periods... I remember crying like crazy one night in my bedroom but I didn't know why, but the next day I came on and I was so happy. I wanted my periods to start because I felt a bit left out as all my friends had theirs. The enthusiasm of having periods soon wore off!! Also it was just awfully stressful relying on carers to keep clean once a month.

In school time, I often would be asked if I wanted to spend time in the art room with Mrs Boyce and I always said yes please. I learnt a lot about the impressionists. I also learnt how to control my head and body enough to paint with my head attachment. I developed a real interest in art from then on.

I would also go to the typing room because Mrs McKaskil wanted me to learn more about the apple computer communication switch access program. One day Mrs McKaskil shut the classroom door and didn't say anything to me. She plugged two foot switches into the apple computer and secured the two switches on a box at my foot height and helped me to manoeuvre my electric wheelchair to them.

She set up the scanning speed and scanning mode. The MAC apple program had a small word prediction list that I would choose from, there were only about 100 words in the prediction lists but this really helped me so much.

Like a duck to water, I was away and couldn't believe how easy I could get my words onto the screen... I think we both saw a little sparkle come into each other's eyes and we could see how computers would be my life line. Not realising how much computers would impact on everything within a few years of my first try of the Apple computer MAC program.

But computers were very expensive for the average person back then; I had to wait a few years to get my own computer.

Student Placements.

The school would often have student carers to do their placement from the spastic society care college in Wallingford, Oxfordshire. The students would come to learn about how to do care work and do case studies. I would often be chosen to be a case study as my disability is quite unusual, as I am severely physically affected but my intellectual capacity isn't affected at all.

I was chosen to be one of the students' case studies this time as I was about to leave school in a few weeks and go to the Princess Marina Centre residential home. The student had been there on a placement and so she got permission to take me to the PMC fete from school. Mum and my sisters came over to meet us there as Beaconsfield is about 24 miles from Borehamwood.

Mum and I were very impressed with the PMC. Mum told Gillian Thursby this on the Monday morning after we had been there.

I always remember this time because I loved (& still do) Spandau Ballet's song "Communication" that was in the charts at the time...

At the age of 19 the lyrics summed up exactly how I felt when people couldn't understand me... Especially the lines

Communication always leaves me incomplete
The grass is greener, but it's grown beneath my feet...
Communication let me down
And I'm left here

A carer at TDS bought me the Spandau Ballet "True" tape as a leaving present.

Over the years, my communication has improved and become easier, mainly because technology is here and I use my feet and eyes for everything.

I still love that song now, and I have said that I would like it played at my funeral just to make people smile.

I finally left school when 1 was 19 and soon went to the Princess Marina centre. I had made some life long friends through out my school life, but I was glad to leave Thomas de la Rue...

In retrospect, I feel that there was too much time given to Physiotherapy for people like me, who in reality couldn't ever be able to walk, talk, undress ourselves but are able to do intellectual tasks.

From my point of view the teaching at Thomas de la Rue school, was not good at all (I can't do number work at all) Mum taught me how to read now 1 think about it. I remember I loved my school work, although I didn't get taught the basic grammar of English, I have only realised this through doing my English Literature later on when I took my English A'leval and being told by my tutors at FE colleges.

As soon as I left school, I went back to using my feet and I am always writing something and communicating with everyone...

It used to be if you can't talk or use your hands, you were almost treated as an experiment at that time and left out of education.

I would hope it's very different for young severely disabled people now, with all the modern technology that is available.

However, if I hadn't have been away from Mum and the family as a whole, I know I wouldn't be as independently minded as I am.

I put this down to wanting to be with my school friends and not being mollycoddled at home. Although I would not have done anything if Mum hadn't have pushed me to do more than anyone thought I'd do.

I still use my head attachment to do art which I enjoy.

7.

The Princess Marina Centre

I left Thomas de la Rue school for the final time in July 1983, and went home for about a month, and then moved into The Princess Marina Centre. The PMC was in Seer Green, near Beaconsfield, Bucks. It was about 30 miles from my family's home in Borehamwood, and about the same mileage from London.

I would have had a formal interview at the Princess Marina Centre after leaving school but I don't remember going for it.

I moved to Seer Green in mid August and there were lots of residents and staff away for the summer holidays.

Mum, Sharon and Michelle took me over to Princess Marina Centre and we were met by a member of care staff, Karen Profett, and shown to my room.

The accommodation for residents was split up into six units attached to a big old country house. I don't know if the house was originally a farmhouse, but there was a barn in the grounds. The Princess Marina Centre was home for about 50 residents.

Karen took us to the unit where my room was in. My room was in the unit called Cedar and it was quite small and very bare, so once Mum had unpacked my case and had given a demonstration of how to feed me to Karen, my family went home. Mum has told me that she was upset when she left me there as she knew I had left home.

I was in the room next to Angela Walse, who had been at school with me; and so I think I spent that first afternoon with her. I didn't feel like I was in an institution because it was very homely and the staff were all nice and friendly.

Mum came back in the evening and brought a few posters, kettle, cups and some tapes.

All the residents were funded to live in the Princess Marina Centre by their home County.

The centre would get money for each resident for rent and food, I don't know how much this was but it was in the thousands. We would get a little bit of spending money out of that. I think our money was about £30pw, so it was a lot to me then, and it was just spending money.

I had my radio cassette with me and for the first time I had access to money, so I bought a lot of cassette tapes over the next 9 years.

There was a good activities program that residents could take part in. The activities ranged from art and crafts, woodwork, English lessons, yoga and other subjects which were organised by a team of ladies and some tutors came in to do various classes. There was also a Speech therapist and Physiotherapist en site, I think they were part time but really did a lot for the residents.

All of the activities were optional and I wasn't used to making my own choices. I decided not to have Physio at first because I didn't see the point of it, after all I had been having Physio since I was 18 months old and I didn't feel I had benefited from it, so I tried yoga as something new.

I did go to Physio again, because I could feel my back twisting through my spasms. The Physio therapist was lovely and talked to me about why my spasms took over and taught me that I needed to be stretched to maintain my body.

I was only 19 and so I wanted to explore the centre. I had my electric wheelchair about three years by then and so I decided to go for a walk round the centre one evening after tea.

I took myself out of Cedar and negotiated the electric doors and negotiated a couple of ramps. I found my way out of the old house and up onto a circular plateau called the Peacock lawn. The back of the old house was surrounded the Peacock lawn and then there was a big lawn that lead down to the drive.

I decided to go around on the path and see the Peacock, which was a big not very inspiring concrete bird in the middle of the circular plateau. Suddenly my front wheel got stuck down in the rut between the circular grass and the path and I couldn't get back out of the rut no matter how I tried. At first

I couldn't see anyone else around, and then I saw a lady in a wheelchair in her room with the door open. So I called out to her and she came over to me. She propelled her wheelchair over with her feet and said in a Geordie accent

Hello, are you stuck?

She had a kind face and a nice smile.

I smiled embarrassed and nodded. The lady then asked my name. She said

I am Pat.. Shall I say the alphabet?

I nodded again and we gradually spelt "Nicki".

Between the two of us, my wheel was pulled out of the rut and we got chatting and became friends. We were to have a lot of fun over the years. Pat was about 16 years older than me so became my confidant as well.

When I first went to the Princess Marina Centre students from Universities came to work there during their holidays. This was great for us residents because they would put on parties and take us out.

There was one group of students from Canterbury University who came regularly for about two years. Their names were Jo, Dave and Paul Kool. Paul is Dutch, has got a lovely accent, quite tall, curly blonde, greying now; hair and has a very nice personality.

There was a communal dining room in the main building, so Pat and I sat together at meal times. We would try getting our favourite carers to feed us and when the students were there we always wanted Paul to feed us! (well I did anyway).

Unfortunately because of my eating difficulties he wasn't allowed to feed me very often.

I can't remember how Paul and I got to know each other. I think it was a gradual mutual admiration and fun loving. Anyway I got to know Paul quite well and we always mucked around together. I remember one summer's afternoon, I was sitting on the Peacock lawn with two of the carers Julie and Carolyn. When all of a sudden Paul appeared behind me, he got me out of my chair and put me over his shoulder and walked off with me! I made out I wanted him to put me down, when really I was loving it! Being small does have its advantages! I remember laughing and wriggling like mad in his arms, and feeling safe.

He eventually put me back in my electric wheelchair and walked off laughing...

He had given me his address and Paul we have kept in touch for years. Although if it hadn't been for Fiona, Paul's wife, I would have lost contact a long time ago due to Paul being a hopeless letter writer!!

A young, gangly fellow came to work as night staff about six months after I had gone to the centre. I can't remember our first encounter but over the years Clive (snotty) Snowden and I became very good friends.

Another favourite care staff of mine at Princess Marina Centre was John Henderson. He was lovely! He was usually dressed scruffy, but he dressed similar to Keith Richards of The rolling Stones; he was quite short, brown hair and eyes, he was really kind to everyone, and had a gorgeous smile. He came from South Shields, Northumbria. I loved his accent and we just clicked.

He would take me into Beaconsfield or High Wycombe on the bus, or we would go down to the pub in Seer Green quite a lot. I soon decided to call him Hendy, as I could say it.

One evening I was in Pat's room and we wanted a drink so Pat pressed the "bleep", within a few minutes "Hendy" came to assist us. The film Superman was on the TV and while our drinks were cooling Hendy decided to get me out of my chair and make out we were flying like "Lowis and Superman"!! I was in absolute hysterics and Pat just cracked up. Pat and I always laughed about the film Superman.

John will always be my Superman, wherever he is!

At Christmas the care staff put on a pantomime for the residents. They were usually a bit tiddly and made it funny.

I can't remember which year it was but they did Sleeping Beauty and guess who Prince Charming was? Yes Hendy!!

All I remember about this pantomime is Hendy running on to the stage with a hobby horse between his legs, with tight black jeans, black waistcoat and a bluey-green shirt on. I looked at Pat, who was sitting beside me, and just smiled a "Oh my God.. He is gorgeous"!! She saw my face and whispered "I know Nicki, I know"..

Then the bit where Prince Charming has to kiss Sleeping Beauty came, the casting was brilliant because Julie Young played Sleeping Beauty. Julie was a lovely lady, really smashing carer and she was pretty, so perfect for the part.

Prince Charming hacked his way through the forest and found Sleeping Beauty and kissed her, and then they fell off the bed!!. The audience erupted into laughter…

Pat could see that there was something between Hendy and I, But I knew he was a care staff and had a girlfriend, so I just enjoyed the little time I had with him.

Wembley.

The Princess Marina Centre was quite close to Wembley and there were always pop concert trips organised for us residents. I became very familiar with Wembley arena.

Living in residential care basically meant I had no responsibilities and so I went to absolutely loads of pop concerts in my first few years at Princess Marina Centre. Including Duran Duran, the Eurythmics and the brilliant Billy Joel!

I also went to see my favourite singer, Paul Young, at Wembley arena for the first time. He was terrific and I have been to him at least 30 times through the years. He was and will always be such a good showman.

Apple Computer.

I was still struggling with my typewriter to write letters to my friends from school and do other writing. I was getting so frustrated because I knew I had been good at typing with my feet at Craig –y- Parc School.

The speech therapist at Princess Marina Centre was like the staff at Craig –y- Parc School, and she believed people should use whatever limb worked best.

My uncle Harold had left a thousand pound each to us three girls, so I decided to put mine to good use. I had to be assessed by the communication specialist team at Charring Cross hospital in 1984 before I bought my Apple Computer. I passed the assessment without a problem. My bedroom was too small and so I had to have my apple computer set up in the library at PMC.

One day a small crowd had gathered to see this new computer being used. Once the man from the hospital had set my foot switches and programmed the scanning speed that I needed, I wrote up on the screen was "My mouth has been unzipped now"!!!

There was a collective groan of "Oh no, what have we let ourselves in for"? Then everyone cheered and laughed with me...

The apple computer really opened a whole new world to me!

One of the activity staff, Tricia Hawes helped me a lot when I first had my Apple computer. I enjoyed being able to write without typing mistakes, although my spelling was terrible and my grammar was atrocious. I could write letters in a day instead of taking about a week, and I started to experiment with different ways of expressing myself.

Being able to do written work quite easily was a bit like being given a car at 17 for an able bodied kid, as it was my independence and I had to learn how to control it and look after the thing. I knew I had to make good use of the new technology but had no idea what to start with.

I can't remember how it came about but I decided I would like to do the Duke of Edinburgh's Award, as I needed something purposeful to work for. I didn't think my English was good enough to do exams at that time because of the frustrating and wasted time at Thomas de la Rue School, so Tricia and I contacted the Duke of Edinburgh's Award officer in Aston Clinton, who came to see me to talk about the scheme.

Fait.

In 1984 Mum, Colin, Sharon and Michelle went on holiday to Rome. It was the first time that Mum had been away without me and so she was feeling guilty.

I didn't mind because I was going to go away with The Young Disabled on Holiday group sometime later that year so I didn't want to go with Mum to Rome.

I have to have my arms put behind me when I eat because they tend to fly about, because of the Athetoid movement; and knock the food on the floor if they aren't. One lunchtime a care staff forgot to put my arms back before putting the food in front of me, and of course my arm knocked the food off of the table. So they had to get me a new lunch... When the new lunch arrived he just put a piece of fish finger in my mouth without checking the temperature first. My mouth clamped shut in spasm and I burnt my mouth on the fish finger!

My mouth is almost constantly moving due to the tongue Thrusts! My mouth was really badly burnt, and every time I moved my tongue it hurt. I couldn't have done anything worse than that, because when I eat my tongue comes forward and it was really sore for months. All the staff were so kind to me, especially Julie, and Marion's night staff team. I had plenty of cuddles from Hendy too.

The first night was so painful that I couldn't sleep, so I think Julie got permission to move my bed into the TV room where the night staff could look after me.

Clive sat with me all night putting ice on my tongue and trying to get water into me, which was very painful but he slowly did it and within a few hours I got some sleep...

Nan Holmes was informed by the staff but I don't remember her coming to see me.. Mum came over when she returned from Rome. Apparently they were in St Peter's Basilica when I had burnt my mouth and Mum had said a prayer for me.

I had booked a holiday in July with the YDH but because my mouth was too bad I had to cancel it. I couldn't eat anything apart from baby food so it was best to cancel it as the volunteer holiday care wouldn't have been enough at that time for me. And I had lost a lot of weight through not being able to eat much.

Oxford club.

As I have said, the staff at PMC were all really good to me. One day, Mary, an SRSW, came to see me and said she knew of a club in Oxford for physically disabled people who were going on holiday to Germany and had a spare place and two helpers free, she thought I might like to meet them. So Mum and I went to meet the organiser Pippa, Sue and Caroline, trainee occupational therapists; in Oxford that weekend. They were really lovely people who said I would be welcome to go to Germany with them.

Before the holiday I had another perm which was supposed to be in a "shaggy dog" style. Unfortunately my hair turned out to be a frizzy mess.

We stayed in a Cologne Youth Hostel, which was quite good and had wheelchair accessible facilities. The food was quite good, although if you asked for steak it was best to say "very well done" or you'd get next to raw meat, I am sure somebody's meat ran off their plate one day!! .

I had a great time with The Club in Cologne and everybody had been interested in how I use my communication board. I had spelt out a few funny things over the holiday and at the end of the holiday I was given a little present... They made an alternative word board for me with all the funny phrases that I and other people had said over the holiday.

I started going to the club sometimes on Monday evenings as I had made friends with some of the people from the holiday in Germany.

I enjoyed going to the Oxford club because it was my escape from PMC. I never invited another resident to come with me.

The club was held in the Duke of Monmouth pub on the Hinksey road. Thinking about it now, the pub wasn't wheelchair accessible really but in those days you just got on with it and made the best of what you had. Also people seemed more willing to help.

Music.

A new rock band hit the charts in 1984 with "Livin' on a Prayer". I quite liked the song and so watched Top of the Pops eagerly!! I couldn't believe the amount of hair the lead singer had!! He had gorgeous long shaggy light brown hair, the tightest jeans I'd ever seen, denim shirt and a gorgeous smile too. It was my first glimpse of Bon-Jovi, and I really started to like that genre of music. I became a Jon-Bon-Jovi fan from then!!

Band Aid and Live Aid.

I remember the autumn of 1984 Michael Buerk, the BBC news reporter, brought the Ethiopian famine to the world's attention. The famine was on a Biblical scale and the film that came out of Ethiopia was horrendous.

Bob Geldof was watching and responded to the BBC news by mobilising the pop world to do something about the images he had seen. With Midge Ure of Ultravox he wrote "Do They Know It's Christmas?" in order to raise money for famine stricken Ethiopia. The song was recorded in Notting Hill by various artists under the name of Band Aid.

I bought the Band Aid single and the 12" single. There was also a video released of the making of the record which one of the staff bought and played on the big screen in the barn. I loved the video because it was of the song being made and none of the singers or musicians were wearing stage clothes... Even Boy George was dressed quite dowdy, with his bright orange hair!!

On 13 July 1985, Geldof and Ure organised Live Aid, a huge event staged simultaneously at the Wembley Stadium in London and John F. Kennedy Stadium in Philadelphia. Due to an unprecedented decision by the BBC to clear its schedules for 16 hours of rock music, the event was also broadcast live in the UK on television and radio.

It was one of the most monumental stage shows in history, with Phil Collins flying on Concorde so that he could play at both Wembley and Philadelphia on the same day.

I went to Live Aid. This was the only concert that the care assistants paid to go to, all the other outings I went on the residents had to pay for the escort as well as themselves. I was quite close to another carer and so Jo-ann escorted me.

I will never forget the Live Aid concert, as I'm sure anyone else who went to either Wembley or Philadelphia won't ever forget it. One of the best bits from my point of view was when Paul Young and Alison Moyet sang together. I don't remember what the song was now, but those two artists were really my favourite singers of the time – and probably of all time!!

Another point that stands out in my memory, and I'm sure anyone who was there will agree; when The Cars song "Drive" video was shown. 80,000 people stood in Wembley stadium in Stunned Silence, watching these horrific images of children starving to death. Thousands upon thousands of skeletons with skin on, just clinging to life!!

The finale was really moving when every artist came on to the stage alongside Paul McCartney and sang "DO THEY

KNOW IT'S CHRISTMAS"! Bob Geldoff was hoisted onto their shoulders to an eruption of applause from 80,000 people in Wembley stadium. The ovation seemed to go on for ages. Until the Wembley council pulled the plug probably around 10.30.

This was about the only time we took the train to go to Wembley and we must have got back to the Princess Marina Centre around 2am and I watched the rest of it on TV. I think I went to bed after dawn because wanted to watch Duran Duran in Philadelphia,

My 21ˢᵗ birthday.

It was my 21st birthday and I had a party in the barn at PMC in the December of 1984. Mum hired the barn for the evening and invited lots of people including Janaki, John, Pippa came from The Oxford club came to it.

I don't think my friends from school Debbie or Kim could make it to this party as the weather is often bad at Christmas.

A few of the residents and staff came to my party like Pat Mitchel and Pedro White. Hendy and Karen gave me a pretty handmade cushion, which I have still got with my treasured things.

Mum, Sharon and Michelle gave me a huge TV/radio/ tape and record player, for my birthday. It had buttons that I could just about operate with my feet, and became quite good at playing my tapes. The volume dial was a bit difficult for me to turn and I would often blast Cedar Unit out! Fortunately the power button was just above the volume dial and I would quickly turn the stereo off.

The Duke of Edinburgh's Award.

HRH The Duke of Edinburgh founded The Duke of Edinburgh's Award in 1956.

The scheme gives young people aged 14-24 the chance to develop skills for life and work, fulfil their potential and have a brighter future.

A DofE programme is a real adventure from beginning to end. It doesn't matter who you are or what your academic and physical abilities are.

There are four sections (five if you're going for Gold) that participants have to complete - Volunteering, Physical, Skills, Expedition and for Gold, a Residential week.

As I was 21 and older than the usual participants starting the Duke of Edinburgh's Award, I went straight into doing the gold Award. This meant I had to do more than other participants doing the gold Award.

Barbara Davies and another lady called Shirley, the south Bucks co-ordinators came to talk to me and Tricia about the Award scheme. I decided that I wanted to do this scheme as it sounded good fun and would show me, and other people; whether or not I could study and achieve anything academically. I knew I wanted to use my brain somehow but I didn't know how to get started.

Tricia also encouraged a few other young residents to do the scheme. We were all around the same age and knew each other from school.

Angela Walse, Mark Urwin and Jane Douglas took the silver level, but we did the basic training as a group so that Tricia could work with me. It wouldn't have been liked if she had just worked with me.

For my skill. I decided to do Creative writing. The scheme doesn't go by how academic you are. You just have to show you can persevere at something and produce a folder that is your own work.

As Seer Green is near Jordans, the Quaker village, I decided to study and write a fictitious story about Quakers. It took me a long time to research and write my first longish story, A Local Legend.

I only had my apple computer with a basic word list to do all my written work with. I had to rely on Tricia and other people to help me research everything.

I also wrote a story about squirrels, an essay about my communication and two poems. I really didn't have a clue how to write good English at this time but I liked being able to write anything and worked at it.

I couldn't write flowing poetry back then and I still have to really try to make my poems rhyme now.

The most difficult requirement to adapt for me was the service section.

Tricia and I had to device other ways for me to be of service.

The centre was renovating one of the living accommodation blocks so that residents could be more independent.

I was asked if I would like to raise some money for this project. I was happy to do this, but I didn't want to just be pushed in my wheelchair and not do much to get the sponsorship. I had my walker that was like a big baby walker; I could put it to good use and I trained for a long time to do a sponsored walk. I gradually built up my distance, I think to start with I only walked about 50 metres then I'd be tired but after around six months I managed to do 1800m in Hinksey Park in Oxford. I raised quite a lot of money and so I split the money between Princess Marina Centre and my social club in Oxford.

Unfortunately, there are some very sad and dishonest people in the world, and quite a lot of money promised never got given to us.

I had been on holiday to Walse and had met Mrs Davis, my speech therapist from Craig –y- Parc School. She was organising a conference about different forms of communication in Cardiff and invited me to go. I wrote a speech on my various ways of communication I had used up until then, which Mrs Davis read out for me. This also went towards my service section.

I also was voted on to the Residents council of Princess Marina Centre, this was taken as part of my service section. I think I did a good job while I was on the council but I found the older residents made the decisions, which was fair enough because I was still quite young and didn't know much about the centre.

One of the council's jobs was to interview new staff. I remember one interview day we had two men called Mike come. They were both really good and came across as right for the job but the older residents didn't think they were really appropriate for care in the residential sector. Pat, my friend, was on the council too. She also thought the Mikes would be good, so we argued the point and won. Fortunately the manager, Steve, agreed that the Mikes were the best candidates and so they got the jobs.

For my physical section I took part in Yoga classes, but as I couldn't do all the positions I studied the history and philosophy of it. I had an excellent tutor and I slowly got the hang of meditation and a few of the positions.

The Princess Marina Centre had an old barn that they restored and used for functions and daily classes. It was a lovely building and had a calming ambiance so was a good place for yoga.

I enjoyed the orienteering part the most because we got out of the centre. While I was learning to map read I went on treks with the others in the group and only did short expeditions from Seer Green.

I was not very good at map reading at first because I couldn't get my head round scaling from the map to what was around me, but I bluffed my way around and don't remember getting very lost.

We had able-bodied participants of the Award to do the expeditions with us so if I couldn't find my way, they would help me a bit, while Tricia and other staff were always quite close by.

While the others in the group only did basic training, I had to do more in depth training and record everything I did. My map reading did improve.

I even learnt a bit of first aid. Although how I'd do it, or tell somebody what to do in an emergency was never actually practiced. Thankfully an emergency situation didn't arise!!

I had to learn about what clothes to wear when you go out on explorations. It was even more important for me to dress in appropriate clothing as when you're a wheelchair user you feel the cold and rain more than able-bodied people.

I did all sorts of orienteering treks in preparation for the final exploration in the August of 1986. I remember one training session I had to do. It was early January and bitterly cold and I had to orienteer around Wendover woods. The ground was frozen solid and it is very hilly in the Chilterns. The volunteers and Mum had to get my wheelchair and I to the summit in something like four hours.

They did it but we were all absolutely frozen and glad to get back to base for hot soup.

Meanwhile, I moved out of the Cedar unit into Gibb house. About three years after he had been on night staff, Clive went onto days and worked in Gibb House.

I was running a bit close to the time limit that I had to complete my Duke of Edinburgh's Award because I was going to be 24 in December 1987 and I still had a lot to do.

I did my practice exploration at Easter in the Lake District and I travelled up in a normal minibus with the able-body participants from Aston Clinton.

I stayed at The Calvert Trust. The Calvert Trust centre is an outside activity centre for disabled people, situated on the shores of Bassenthwaite Lake, in the heart of the Lake District National Park

There are three Calvert Trust centres in England and I have been to all of them, but my favourite was the Lake District.

Clive was the only person mad enough to come with me. We shared a room and I felt completely safe. One morning he got up from his bed, thinking I was asleep, and had lime green under pants on!! The next thing Clive saw were my eyes peeping over my quilt absolutely creased up!! I told everyone at Princess Marina Centre about this!

One evening we were listening to the radio and The Beatles song "Let it be" was played. I was relaxed and giggling and suddenly I came out with "Ooh aah ding ding"! Clive cracked up and said "McCartney couldn't have written lyrics like that, Nicki"! I always laugh now when I hear "Let It Be".

I had never been to the North of England before this and I didn't know what to expect. I loved the Lake District, with it's beautiful countryside of mountains and lakes.

The Aston Clinton group were going to do their final expedition in Cumbria and so Shirley and the other assessors wanted me to do my final exploration near them, to make it easier to watch me.

One of the days I joined the group as they were doing rock climbing and the leaders decided I should experience climbing too.

I had to wait for The Calvert Trust staff to take me in their minibus to Ambleside to meet up with the able-bodied participants. About six strong young men had already secured ropes and pulleys to a rock face and got a harness to fix me into my wheelchair more securely, and once I was secure onto the ropes they slowly manhandled my wheelchair up the rock. It was brilliant and I loved it! The weather was bright sunshine and the views over Ambleside were amazing! Some of The Calvert Trust staff came to the group and they abseiled me back down. I think Clive also abseiled after me!

It was the best Easter weekend that I had!

I did my final exploration in August at The Calvert Trust. I had a girl called Laura for my carer, and two Duke of Edinburgh's Award participants who were doing their residential week, to help me.

As I have always liked birding I decided to study the bird life around Bassenthwaite Lake and the surrounding area. I had a tape of birdsong; I think it had about 20 different birdsong on. I spent weeks listening to this tape. It must have driven everyone in Gibb house mad!! I was tested on how many birdsongs I recognised by a man in Keswick, and I think I recognised around 16!! I couldn't do that now!!

Things were so different back then. Carers could do anything and take disabled people anywhere they wanted. They just had to tell the person who was in charge and be sensible. These days, I couldn't have done half the things I did in 1986, because of the health and safety laws in care... I am so glad I was born in the 1960's.

One day we hiked up on Skidaw, which is the mountain behind The Calvert Trust. This was quite a trek for anyone, let for alone a wheelchair-bound person. The three young people slowly got me up the steep incline of the mountain. As it was all up quite steep hill my wheelchair was attached to ropes with Karabiners. I slowly ascended part way up Skidaw. I can't remember how far up we got. We had lunch beside a stream and I saw a Dipper, I was very happy to see this bird because they only populate very quiet places.

After lunch, Laura assisted me to get out of my wheelchair and helped me to walk on the mountain a little bit, which sort of made my expedition complete.. This is my favourite memory of my Duke of Edinburgh's Award experience. The week expedition ended all too soon at The Calvert Trust but to celebrate I camped along with the group from Aston Clinton on the last night,

I did my Residential week in Trier, West Germany. A man from the DoE scheme drove the mini bus from the PMC to Trier.

Because Tricia couldn't just take me away the others had to come with me but I planned it all. Tricia and I found three able-bodied people who were doing their Duke of Edinburgh's Award residential week to come with us and help with our care, guided by Tricia. I made friends with a young lady called Racheal. We got on well over the week and kept in touch for a while after. We stayed in two wooden chalets surrounded by forest and we had to cook for ourselves.

I can't remember the purpose of going to Trier but we went to a reception with the Mayor of Trier and some German youngsters.

The Duke of Edinburgh's Award scheme published a book to encourage disabled youngsters to do the scheme. As we were amongst the first severely disabled youngsters to do the Award, the organisers decided that we should have our pictures taken to go into the book. The photo shoot took place on the philanthropist Paul Gettie's estate at Stokenchurch, and Princess Marina Centre, it was a long day. A few months later I went to the book launch. Prince Edward was at the launch.

I hope young severe physically disabled people still have the opportunity to participate fully in The Duke of Edinburgh's Award scheme, as it was a major springboard for me.

On December 1st 1987 Mum, Tricia Hawes and I went to St James' Palace to be presented with the award by The Duke! The dress code for the occasion was suits and ties for men, and dresses for women. I didn't wear dresses often because my hands tend to grab the skirt and show everything! So we had to get permission for me to wear culottes from the palace because I really didn't want to be embarrassed by flashing at The Duke. I finally received permission a week before the day and Mum made a lovely black velvet culotte suit for me.

After the Award ceremony, Mum treated Tricia, Barbara and Shirley and I to afternoon tea at The London Hilton.

I completed the Duke of Edinburgh's Award the same year as Prince Edward...

I took four years to do the Duke of Edinburgh's Award, and I loved everything I did for it. I gained the confidence to go to able-bodied College to do my GCSEs, A'leval and countless other things in life generally.

Memorable year.

I remember one particular year for so many reasons, mostly happy but some sad. I was 21 in late 1984 and had an eventful 1985.

Steve Barnard, the PMC manager, had previously worked at another residential centre in Perth, Scotland, and an exchange program had started between the two centres. One of the care staff, Carolyn, had been up there on the last trip and got friendly with a member of the care staff. Ross came down to Princess Marina Centre to see her and she brought him round to see the centre. I was sitting in the garden as they were passing through so she introduced us... He was quite good looking so when the next trip to Upper-Springlands was put on the chalkboard, Pat and I were the first to put our name down.

Upper Springlands residential centre was on the bank of the river Tay in Perthshire, Scotland. It was very modern and had flats instead of just bedrooms and communal toilet facilities like PMC had.

This was my first trip to Scotland and I enjoyed travelling around when we went out on trips. I particularly liked Edinburgh, with all of its old buildings and imposing castle. On the last night we went to a nightclub in Perth and some people from Upper Springlands came along too, accompanied by Ross. I was so happy and decided I was going to have a dance out of my chair with him. I'd told the carer that was with us that if Madonna's "Crazy for you" was played to get Ross for me. I think he did get me out of my chair and he gave me his address and I wrote to him when I got back. He didn't write back the rat...

Hendy.

Hendy had a long term girlfriend called Karen who was really nice, and I liked her a lot. She fell pregnant and had a girl who they called Kiersten, after a Danish care staff. I wrote my first children's story for little Kiersten.

John and Karen got married in August of 1985, I think in South Shields, I was happy for them, even though I knew I really cared for him deeply. However, being a realist, I didn't say or do anything to stop them getting married. Also I knew that Karen really was his true love.

I remember on their wedding day, I stayed in my room playing tapes all day and I was very glum. Only Pat knew why I was a moody cow that day.

John and Karen and baby Kiersten came back to PMC for a few weeks before they moved to Liverpool so that John could do his PE teacher training. Once or twice Hendy let me watch over little Kiersten for a few minutes, she was always asleep and I'd panic if she stirred. Hendy would always come back and see my panicked face, even though baby Kiersten was perfectly OK.

I think I realised about this time that I didn't want my own children because I can't look after them, as much as I love children.

It was the summer holidays and trips out were put on each day, and Hendy asked if I would like to go to Windsor before he left. We had a lovely day together. He treated me to a boat trip along The Thames, we had a pub lunch and he gave me The Go West tape, which I really liked at the time.

In the evening he took me swimming and in the Jacuzzi at PMC. He was the perfect gentleman! I felt completely safe with him. I went to bed a very happy young lady that night, although I knew I would lose him soon.

The day before they left, I had to give John his leaving present from the centre, which was horrible but Paul Sowerby asked me specifically to do the presentation because he knew John was fond of me.

The presentation took place in the dining room so people could gather and show their appreciation. I zoomed up to John with the present and tried to zoom off again but Paul switched my electric wheelchair off so John could give me a thank you kiss.

The dreaded day came all too soon, when John left Princess Marina Centre. Pat and I went out to the car park where John and Karen's removal van was loaded and ready to go to Liverpool. I tried to hide behind Pat's wheelchair because I knew I would cry when John said goodbye to me. It didn't work because he saw me and ran over to me and gave me a big hug and kissed me, and then was gone.... That was the first time I felt my heart break by losing John.

We kept in touch for a few years after but it petered out, I think they moved around a lot. He qualified as a PE teacher. John got called George Michael by the girls at his school. This would have been the worst insult imaginable to John because he hated Wham! I cracked up when that letter came. I can imagine him saying in his Geordie accent "George Michael? Ffff ing ell"!

He sent me a postcard with Paul Young on, which I keep in my box of treasures. I never expected to treasure these times so much…

Club Holiday.

Pippa had left Oxford and so John Hemmett took over the running of the club. One of the trips he organised was to The Royal Tournament, at Earls Court in London. Obviously I went along to see the horses.. The fact that there were hundreds of soldiers all in uniform didn't interest me, not much!! My eyes couldn't believe their luck!! One of the helpers told me that there would be some new helpers going on holiday to Wales with us, and a couple of young fellows at that!! I think I just laughed.

The day after Hendy left, I went on holiday to Wales. Mum and I drove up to Oxford one Saturday in late August to meet everyone from the club. We met in the grounds of The Churchill Hospital in Headington, Oxford, where we all got onto a coach which was adapted to take wheelchairs. John Hemmett had said I could take my new Vessa electric wheelchair on holiday. I had only had the chair a few weeks and I wasn't very accurate with it. I zigzagged over to the coach. All of a sudden, this bloke came sauntering up and said something derogative about my driving... I had never met him before and I remember giving him a filthy look...

After a five-hour journey, we arrived at the youth hostel in Haverfordwest, in Pembrokeshire. After dinner we went to the local pub where I talked to Alan, who had been with us in Germany; to start with. After a while curiosity got the better of me because this poor bloke was sitting at the bar, looking like a fart in a trance. He had obviously not had much contact with disabled people and so I asked Alan who he was... He was a work mate of Alan's and his name was Malcolm Hart. Alan called him over and introduced us to one another.... Malcolm was a tall, 22-year-old, short neat brown-haired, blue eyed chap. The total opposite to Hendy, but he was quite cute.

Alan showed Malcolm how I use my communication board and he just let the conversation flow. Over the next few days Malcolm had no difficulty learning how to understand my eyes. Funnily enough he became expert on when I was cheeky very quickly, I can't imagine why!

John had organised lots of trips over the week to various places around Haverfordwest. On the nice days we went on sight seeing trips

We went to the cinema one rainy afternoon to see the Living Daylights, James Bond film. I think one of the older ladies had taken a bit of a shine to Malcolm (he was a little bit nervous of her) and so he asked to sit with me. Whilst we were waiting for the film to start, Malcolm said he'd got a "Silver tongue. You know what that means, Nicki"? I nodded and looked at him wryly then spelt out "Sweet talker"! (I would never have guessed that!!!)

On another day, I was accosted by Morris men at a pub which amused the group immensely; John Hemmett got me out of my wheelchair and stood with me while they danced around me. It was so embarrassing but funny.

We went to Tenby one day and Malcolm took me for a drink on our own. This must have been really daunting for him because I am not easy to feed at the best of times and when I'm excited/nervous it's even harder, but we got through it and got on really well and we took quite a shine to each other over the week's holiday.

We visited a little Welsh craft shop and saw the tradition of Love-spoon making. A Love-spoon is a wooden spoon decoratively carved that was traditionally presented as a gift of romantic intent. For tourists these days they carve names into the dip of the spoon...

I told Janaki I would like to get Malcolm a spoon just as a little present for making my holiday fun and I thought a lot of him.

I was very surprised when Malcolm and I exchanged love-spoons.

Apart from Hendy and Clive, who were staff and couldn't be "a friend", Malcolm was the first able-bodied man (apart from family) that could show affection for me. A couple of evenings on that holiday, after going to the pub, he would talk with everybody in the communal area. He was quite strong and would often pick me up out of my wheelchair and sit me on his lap and we would talk. If people drifted away and Janaki (my friend and carer on that holiday) was doing something, he would cuddle and kiss me like I had never experienced before. Nothing sexual ever happened! We just enjoyed being with each other!! I was a young severely disabled lady and I was really flattered!!

All good times come to an end and the holiday's last morning arrived...

After breakfast we went outside the youth hostel to get onto the coach and as I was one of the last people to get loaded on, I took myself around the corner of the youth hostel to see the sea and think for a little while.

I knew I liked Malcolm a lot but I also knew that he had a very different life from mine and so I thought we would not see one another much after the holiday. A little while after I had wandered away from the coach, I was joined by Malcolm. He sensed I was feeling uncertain about him and after the holiday so he asked if we could keep in touch. Remembering what happened with Ross I said "Yes, but you write to me first!!"

All good times come to an end and the holiday's last morning arrived...

After breakfast we went outside the youth hostel to get onto the coach and as I was one of the last people to get loaded on, I took myself around the corner of the youth hostel to see the sea and think for a little while.

I knew I liked Malcolm a lot but I also knew that he had a very different life from mine and so I thought we would not see one another much after the holiday. A little while after I had wandered away from the coach, I was joined by Malcolm. He sensed I was feeling uncertain about him and after the holiday so he asked if we could keep in touch. Remembering what happened with Ross I said yes but you write to me first!!

I went back to the Princess Marina Centre and just got on with the Duke of Edinburgh's Award scheme. I missed Hendy dreadfully but I knew that he was going to be great as a PE teacher and Dad, so I pushed him to the back of my mind.

Malcolm wrote to me about a fortnight later and came down from Oxford to Beaconsfield to see me every week.

I would go to that Oxford club whenever I could. It was run on every other Monday and Mum would usually take me, or I would get a member of staff to do the 100 mile round trip...

My friend Pat had to go to the Churchill hospital in Headington, Oxford, I had told her about Malcolm and I know she was waiting for it to change because she had been in that situation years before.

Pat and her boyfriend had been invited to a church function in Oxford and asked if I would like to share the cost of the transport and spend an evening with Malcolm.

Obviously I jumped at the opportunity and arranged to meet him at the Churchill.

We went to Malcolm lodgings for the evening. I was so happy because I was with him alone. I didn't feel nervous or worried at all. I became aware that although he loved me for me, he didn't want a full on relationship with me. This was really difficult for me at the age of 21 to accept, because I was a young woman who wanted this young man that was paying me so much attention. It was confusing but I kept myself in check and we decided to become close friends from then.

Life at home.

Life for Mum had been pretty weird since Dad died, and I don't know the half of it. Mum and Colin had got married in the May 1985. She looked lovely in her pink and blue suit. She was working at a Milliner and made her own hat.

Sharon and her then boyfriend Boyd decided to go to Australia for a year's working holiday. Before they went I took Malcolm home to meet my family. Sharon didn't like him and warned him off me, not realising that we had already determined it was only ever going to be friendship. She was only trying to protect me, as she had always done; she just didn't realise that Malcolm and I had already talked about the future, even though that decision was hard for me at that time.

The day that Sharon and Boyd flew to Australia for a year arrived. Everything changed from that day on.

The whole family went to Heathrow airport to see them off. I remember trying not to cry when they went through to departure because it would upset Mum, Nanny Conway and Michelle.

Boyd came back after a month or so, but Sharon coped, so he left her out there, and she met people.

Not long after Sharon went Mum's house was burgled. We had two dogs at the time Zoe, Sharon's Labrador, and Hen my little Yorkie. They were let out of the garden by whoever it was burgled us. Zoe was found outside the butcher's shop and was quite happy. But sadly little Hen was killed. We think she had a heart attack because somebody found her beside the road and there wasn't a mark on her.

I was at the Princess Marina Centre when the burglary happened and so Mum had to come over to tell me about Hen. I was very upset.

We think someone had been put up to the job because they knew what they wanted and where to look even though Mum had hidden all the jewellery. They just took all our Christening bracelets, charm bracelets, lots of inherited jewellery. And sadly the worst thing that was taken was Dad's wedding ring.

Gladstonbury.

A group of residents and staff went to Gladstonbury every year near the summer solstice. I had wanted to go for years and this year, 1986; Karen Profett asked me if I wanted to go with her. She knew my answer was going to be yes because we had become friends and we had talked about it...

I can't remember a lot about this weekend. Apart from I had a load of coffee so that I could stay awake all night. I think we left the guesthouse around 2.30am and walked to the start of the long hill up to the Tor. The slopes of the hill are terraced, but the method by which they were formed remains unexplained.

I must have been the only resident that year to want to see the sunrise because the 4 staff helped Jim Read carry me the terraced hill.

We got to the Tor before sunrise and it was awesome to see the land slowly getting lighter all around, the dawn chorus get louder and finally see the sun break over the horizon flooding people earth in a golden light and warmth...

I had never seen anything so beautiful before, and very few things as beautiful since!

Gibb House.

In March 1986, as well as finishing the last bits of my Duke of Edinburgh's Award, I moved out of Cedar Unit and over to Gibb house, which was a separate building from the main centre. Gibb house, AKA the hostel; had just been renovated and the theory of the hostel was to encourage the residents to lead as independent lives as possible. There were about ten residents living in Gibb house and there were communal toilets, bathrooms and a kitchen/laundry. A couple of the residents could do everything for themselves but we also had four senior staff and there were about ten CSVs (community service volunteers) that worked shifts and provided the care around the clock.

We had to book when we wanted the carers to assist us, and we were not allowed to stipulate male or female carers. I absolutely hated having the young male CSVs doing my personal care, especially when I was menstruating! The policy of the centre was that there was no difference between male and female carers, as they were just doing a job!! I had so many arguments with the senior care staff about that because it was embarrassing for both carer and me. The reason that they gave was that I wouldn't be able to choose the carer's sex when I moved out of care. I have found out that this was not necessarily true because it's a safeguarding issue. If a woman is vulnerable in their home, male carers are not supposed to go into them unaccompanied. Unless the female client specifically say otherwise.

Many residents went to Milton Keynes from Princess Marina Centre; One of the SRSWs tried to persuade me to go to Milton Keynes because of the Spastic Society's set-up at Neath Hill, a sheltered living scheme with care on hand. This would have been good but it would have been too far away from Mum and the family. The number of rows I had over this issue was ridiculous. I'm glad I stuck to my guns on this. The SRSW of Gibb house even suggested I live with Pedro White once... I don't remember my exact reply but I think it along the lines of "P" and ended with "OFF"!!!!

I am glad I stuck to my guns on this!!

Home Life.

Sharon only had a year's working visa for Australia and so she came home. She had met an Australian man and so he came back with her to meet her family and do a year's work here. His name was Neil. Cameron. They landed just as the hurricane of October 1987 hit middle England. The Australian was tall and strong as he was a miner and so Neil chopped up the Willow tree that fell in Mum's garden and he thought that we always had hurricanes.

They got engaged on Sharon's 21st birthday and a year later Sharon immigrated to Australia. I don't know how much this upset Mum. I know it really upset me and I know Michelle really felt the loss terribly...

Oxford club.

I decided to stop going to the Oxford club, because there was only Malcolm going who I was friendly with. At the end of every club evening Malcolm would always put me in the car and we would always have a chat and a cuddle.

He said he'd come down and see me every month, which he did until I left the centre in 92...

8.

Time To Move On.

In 1989 The Princess Marina Centre adapted three bed rooms in the old house and made them into bed-sits, with kitchenettes and showers/toilets in. I moved into one of the bed-sits, which gave me a bit more independence, not physically but mentally. I had the money for food as well as my ordinary pocket money and so I started buying all my own food, cleaning products and was virtually living independently, but still within the shelter of the residential home sector.

Also with the constant threat of closure by Scope the morale of the staff was very low, and most of my favourite care staff and all of my friends who were residents, had left.

A few months passed I begun to feel I needed to move out of residential care all together as I had been at The Princess Marina Centre for six years by then.

I had been through all of the "independence training" and was starting to think of my next options.

I hadn't been contacted by a social worker from Herts in that time. So wanting to move out of The Princess Marina Centre I wrote asking who my social worker was, explaining I wanted to move. Within a week of sending the letter I was visited by the head Occupational Therapist and my new social worker from St Albans, because this was where Mum lived.

I always have to have somebody with me to assist with my communication when I first meet someone. One particular visit, the only member of staff they would let me have was Eileen, a CSV. Actually looking back she was probably the most qualified member of staff in the place left, certainly the most sensible. (Murphy sat on her back though)

Everything we asked the OT she would say, "I don't know". She wouldn't find out about anything for me. In my naivety I offered to write letters to housing associations, St Albans council, care agencies etc. She didn't even get the addresses for me... I asked about care help, she said about home care, "They go in to my ladies once a week to clean". Eileen and I looked at each other in total disbelief because she didn't offer any alternatives or suggestions. Then she asked Eileen if she wanted to be my carer! "No thanks, I'm going to Germany to teach when my six months are up here", was Eileen's quick reply! (She had a diploma in teaching; she was a very brainy woman but a total scatter brain too).

After the OT went I got a bit upset because I was getting nowhere. I think Eileen took me down to the pub that evening.

My St Albans social worker arranged a meeting at Princess Marina Centre, the home care managers came to say what they could offer. The meeting was a total farce! The social worker for the spastic society spoke for me. It was decided that St Albans were going to send home carers over to Princess Marina Centre for a month to learn how to care for me. The fact that there was a different layout in the bed-sit to the flat didn't seem to register.

By 1991 I wasn't getting anywhere with my flat business and the stress was starting to show, I lost weight and I was thin anyway, but I couldn't eat. I was so pissed off with the Princess Marina Centre.

There were going to be local elections in May. I was on council list but they wouldn't house me until my care package, the OT wasn't doing anything to get care. Mum suggested I wrote to the St Albans housing officer asking for an interview. I said I knew this wasn't the usual way but nor was my case. With no word of a lie, within six weeks I was offered two flats, one in St Albans and one in London Colney that was being built! I had to give a St Albans address as a contact address. Mum got the letter and phoned me up! I freaked out with excitement! Mum brought the letter over to me that evening. I decided to wait for the London Colney flat to be built.

The Outsiders Club.

Some of the residents went to a social club in London called The Outsiders Club. The name didn't appeal to me so I didn't go with them. The activity staff organised a party and invited the Outsiders club!

I didn't bother getting dressed up as there was no point as it was only at Princess Marina Centre! Late in the evening this man rolled up! Mmm I thought, but another resident had captured him. I was sitting quite close to Debbie and this fellow and I could hear snippets of the conversation, he said something funny and I laughed, he saw me and smiled. Eventually she moved away and I drove a bit closer to him, I think he then came to talk to me. I got Trish to help me to talk to him with my board. It didn't take him long to get the hang of it and we got on really well. I had to go down to my room at 12:00 because the hostel's evening staff went off at 1:00. I got Colin's address and went. About an hour after I had gone to bed there was a knock on my door, it was a member of staff with Colin wanting to say goodbye properly... Colin had a good sense of humour that saw us through good and bad times, both at Princess Marina Centre and when I moved to London Colney.

Colin was from Barking, Essex. He was funny and he had Muscular Dystrophy. He drove a Bedford van which he had designed a way of getting into himself. He was a design engineer so he made the side of the Bedford van open downwards so it became his ramp into the Bedford van, he would attach a pully to his wheelchair and he had a button that would start a winch system that pulled him into the Bedford van!! It was amazing and in common use now.

Australia.

I think it was February 1990, Mum and I went to Australia to see Sharon and Neil. I also took a carer with me because it was too much for Mum to do everything for me for a month. I loved it there. It was so laid back, sunny and hot. Sharon and Neil lived in an old, wooden bungalow overlooking the ocean. Their back stairs lead down to Austimer beach which is on the Tasmanian Sea, and about 60 miles South of Sydney.

We did a lot of sightseeing trip over the three weeks holiday. Sydney aquarium was pretty good because it has a glass tunnel that goes out under the sea, which is really clear and the fishes are all around you.

One weekend we did a road trip to The Blue Mountain, and saw the rock formation called The Three Sisters. I remember looking over the viewpoint and there was nothing but Bush and mountains for miles around.

We went through a tunnel that had been carved through the mountain by hand by convicts from Europe. It was about 15ft high and probably 50ft long.

We stayed in a motel somewhere near Wombeyan caves, which was interesting because a fight broke out in the pub next door. A woman smashed a bar stalls over a man's head at one point. Fortunately Neil had told Dorte to get me out of the pub before it kicked off.

The next day we went to the Wombeyan caves. They are partially in The Blue Mountain National Park, and were not wheelchair accessible at all. Luckily Neil was pretty tall and strong and so he carried me round. Some places were really narrow and Neil had to threadle me through the gap to Sharon and then squeezed himself through.

On the way back to Austimer Neil suddenly stopped the car because there was a snake in the middle of the bloody road. It was long, black and looked horrible. I really have a fear of snakes so I stayed in the car, even though it was dead. I gladly let Neil move it and the rest looked at it... I didn't care how rare it was!!

We were in Australia for three weeks and I enjoyed the holiday but I missed my electric wheelchair, computer and Colin.

G.C.S.Es

I had been doing a little amount of painting with my head attachment and so I enrolled in art classes. I must have shown potential as the tutor suggested I try using acrylic paint. I liked different effects I could get with acrylics and I decided I would like to do my art GCSE in 1990. The course work was marked by the teacher at Beaconsfield Girls School. They adapted the course work a little bit because I couldn't physically do the technical drawing part and so the examiners marked my paintings and a project about water. I got an A grade art GCSE.

I decided that I wanted to go to Amersham college to do my English GCSE in September 1990. This was a big leap for me as I'd never been in classes with able-bodied people. The college arranged for a lady to help me to take notes in class and I'd type the essays up, in my own time at PMC.

I sat my GCSE English language in May of 1991. I was allowed to take the exam paper in my bed-sit because my adapted Apple computer was set up there. The College sent an invigilator to sit in with me to make sure I did the exam without any help. Tricia was sitting outside my bed-sit in case I needed anything.

There was a lot of building work happening quite near my bed-sit and all of sudden someone turned off the electricity just as I started writing the exam paper in the afternoon of my first exam. I was in a total panic. The invigilator called Tricia into my bed-sit.

All hell broke out because the builders would not put the electric back on. In the end I think Greg, the IT guy, phoned Park Crescent (the Spastic society's head office) and had a go at them. The builders had a schedule to get work done and they didn't realise that I was doing a seven hour exam! The electric was eventually put on again and I finished the exam at about seven o'clock that evening. I was knackered for about a week after. I resat the exam in the November and managed to get a C grade for my English language GCSE.

I decided to do Child Psychology GCSE the next year but I didn't understand any of it because my brain isn't sociologically inclined. Nevertheless I received a D grade because I didn't sit the exam. I just did the course work because I was so worn out after sitting my English GCSE.

Nanny Conway.

In the October of 1990. Nanny Conway was diagnosed as having bowel cancer. This was a huge shock to everybody because Nanny had never drunk or smoked her only vice was bingo and she didn't win often.

Sharon came back from Australia for a fortnight to see Nan, while she was still fairly well. It was awful seeing Nan in so much pain and just fading away. The last time Michelle and I saw her was on Boxing Day and she died on New Year Eve's morning.

When I found out that Nan had cancer and hadn't long to live, I made a conscious decision to go to the funeral and get over my fear of them. Early January 1991, the lovely person Christian Conway was laid to rest in Dunstable cemetery. I didn't cry until they lowered the coffin into the grave. I'm glad I went to it as it was closure for me.

Back to Australia.

I had a phone put into my bed sit because it was a nuisance having to use the communal telephones and it got me used to having a monthly bill to pay. One morning in about May 1991, Sharon rang, from Australia, to say she was pregnant, I was so happy!!

Mum and I left for Australia on 24th December, 1991, from Gatwick. The cheapest flights we could get were on Christmas Eve and we had a 14 hour stop over in Hong-Kong airport. We couldn't afford to book a room in a hotel for the stopover so we stayed in the airport. Needless to say we got to Sharon and Neil's on December 26th, absolutely knackered. Sharon was hugely pregnant and looked like a pear drop on legs!

It was really weird having my birthday in the sunshine, as it was on 27th. We had a barbecue and a swim.

Mum and I were disappointed as it rained on New Year's Eve, but we sat on the veranda and watched people swim in the sea.

I decided that because we couldn't afford to pay for a carer to come with us I would spend some time in a residential care centre, so Mum could help Sharon had the baby.

Sharon found a residential centre in Fairy Meadow which was near Austimer. It was mainly for learning disability people but the staff were all really lovely to me. They organised lots of trips for me. I must have said I wanted to meet a beach lifeguard because one day I was taken on a tour of beaches!!

There was a really lovely carer called Margaret who I got on well with. She knew some very nice lifeguards!!

Sharon had Karah on January 7th 1992, at Woolongong hospital NSW, Australia. I went to see my first little niece a day later. Sharon called her baby girl Karah Jacqueline Cameron.

At the end of January 1992, Mum and I returned from Australia,

It was an awful feeling as we drove up Princess Marina Centre's drive. It was a Saturday morning, Mum and I had just had a 36 hour flight back from Australia, it was cold and dull and Princess Marina Centre looked so forbidding to me! I cried bitterly as Mum took me in! I hated that place on that day. We walked into my room and it really was like walking into a rubbish tip, as there were half packed boxes everywhere! I can't describe my feelings. All I knew was that I wanted to get out of there pretty damn quick!! I was made to feel really welcome too (I jest), nobody but nobody came to say hello to me all morning… I can't remember who did my lunch but I don't think I was even asked whether I had had a nice holiday, it was only on the Monday morning that I had the chance to tell somebody about my holiday. I think Tricia, Margaret and Ann (the activities staff) were the first people I talked to.

First thing Monday morning 3rd Feb, Mum rang St Albans social services to see what was happening about my care programme. The OT had done nothing.

Malcolm.

In August 1991 Malcolm came to see me one evening, I knew there was something unusual about him but I wasn't sure what! He said that he had met a girl called Helen, (I rolled my eyes, another one I thought) but he had a twinkle in his eyes I had never seen in him before. I was hoping to get tickets to see Bryan Adams and knowing Malcolm liked him, I asked him if he would like to come with me. The answer was "yes, can you get three tickets, my friend would like to come too"...

Unfortunately I didn't get tickets for that concert, but Malcolm brought Helen to see me the next month,

About a week after I had returned from Australia, Malcolm came to see me... He said he had something to tell me, and it was going to change things a little bit with our friendship. Of course, I had my suspicions since before I went to Australia, having met Helen...

I think he was nervous about my reaction to his announcement, but I had an idea what he was going to say.

We sat in my bed sit, beside each other just chatting about Sharon and Karah, Australia and everything I had done out there.. I could see he didn't know how to get on to the subject of Helen and so I asked how she was...

"Er.. She's great thanks... We really get on terrific.. Actually, Nicki, we are thinking of Helen moving in to my flat. My sister is getting married soon and it just makes sense"...

I had to really fight my emotions and give him a smile and signal to him that I was happy for him, which I was, but I had really strong feelings for him still. But even deeper than these feelings, I knew that he had to get married to somebody else because that was something we had always known would happen.

I think I asked for a hug and spelt out, "I had a feeling this was going to happen. You have never brought a lady to meet me before".

I was glad to get to bed that night!! I think I had a few tears to myself even though I was happy for Malcolm.

Going Home.

I left The Princess Marina Centre on March 10th 1992 and came to my new home in London Colney, Hertfordshire.

Mum moved all my belongings over in her car, and I don't remember anyone seeing me off.

Mum had a quandary, she didn't want me to move out of residential care but the care at PMC had really deteriorated.

Not long before I was due to leave, Mum came over one evening to visit me and help me do some packing ready to move.

I was getting very nervous about moving and I was in the middle of a migraine. I had been put into bed and I had been sick. I had pressed the "bleep" to get help about 15 minutes before Mum got there and they eventually came to see to me about half hour after that, by which time Mum had cleaned me up. I was able to turn on to my side, luckily.

I was ready to take the biggest risk of my life and really didn't have a clue what I was going to encounter next.

Reference Page.

Credits

www.conductive-education.org.uk
From Wikipedia, the free encyclopedia
https://en.wikipedia.org/wiki/Conductive_education

Scope
www.scope.org.uk

Jumbulance Holidays
Unit 42,
Thrales End Farm,
Thrales End Lane,
Harpenden,
AL5 3NS
01582 765423
Craig-Y-Parc School
Heol Y Parc
Pentyrch

CARDIFF
CF15 9PD
029 2089 0397

The Duke of Edinburgh's Award
https://www.dofe.org

Spandau Ballet lyrics
https://www.azlyrics.com/lyrics/spandauballet/
communication.html

Band Aid and Live Aid research
https://en.wikipedia.org/wiki/Band_Aid_(band)
https://en.wikipedia.org/wiki/Live_Aid

An explanation of Cerebral Palsy can be found at
https://www.cerebralpalsy.org/about-cerebral-palsy/
definition

CPSIA information can be obtained
at www.ICGtesting.com
Printed in the USA
BVHW031631250821
615141BV00005B/59